RANGERS
101

A POCKET GUIDE IN 101 MOMENTS, OBJECTS, CHARACTERS AND GAMES

TOMMY McINTYRE

POLARIS
PUBLISHING

This edition first published in 2021 by

POLARIS PUBLISHING LTD
c/o Aberdein Considine
2nd Floor, Elder House
Multrees Walk
Edinburgh, EH1 3DX

Distributed by
Birlinn Limited

www.polarispublishing.com

ISBN: 9781913538545
eBook ISBN: 9781913538552

British Library Cataloguing-in-Publication Data
A catalogue record for this book is available on request from the British Library.

Designed and typeset by Polaris Publishing, Edinburgh

Printed in Great Britain by MBM Print SCS Limited, East Kilbride

For Tara & Morven, let your story be just as glorious.

ACKNOWLEDGEMENTS

I owe a debt of gratitude to those who have supported me throughout this book, to Polaris Publishing, the Mitchell Library in Glasgow, to the authors who have come before and to those who opened their ears, doors and archives to me. I also offer my thanks to the global community that is the Rangers family. But first and foremost, my thanks go to the four young men who started all of this, without them there would be no club, no support, no story: no book.

INTRODUCTION

As I write this, Rangers Football Club approach their 150th year of existence, proudly sitting as current Scottish champions. Fresh from the fire of liquidation the club and support have shown the character and community mould which is its lifeblood can be tested in the white-hot heat of mismanagement and envy but will not crack.

Where does the recent 55th league win sit in the history of the club? Only time will tell, and I look forward to being part of debates and chats about that in bars, restaurants and terraces until the great referee calls time on my game.

The past is a helpful lens through which to view the present, a much-needed giver of perspective in an ever-trigger-happy world. This book seeks to provide some of that history (both far and near) via statistics, characters, matches and objects. I have attempted to give a flavour of the people who have shaped this institution as well as some of the highs and lows which thread through its story since that mythical day in 1872 to now. Some are more irreverent than others.

All choices on inclusion have been mine and inevitably my fellow fans will have differing views. 'Why isn't "The Iron Curtain"' defence in there?' Or 'How could you leave out Rangers' forlorn attempt at a basketball team?' 'And while you are at it, where the hell is Hamed Namouchi?'

There are so many that didn't make the cut that I have often found myself passionately arguing against my own selections late into the night. It may be that a single volume is not enough for such a storied club. But here they are, my selection, my 101 snapshots across the landscape of time, tragedy and silverware which come to mind when I am asked about Rangers. I look forward to readers suggesting their own alternatives; there are no right or wrong views.

Tommy McIntyre
October 2021

1

Four Lads Had a Dream

All stories have a beginning, so much is true. But from a penniless dream of four wee boys to a global name, only the Rangers have that.

Moses and Peter McNeil, Peter Campbell and William McBeath were enjoying a friends' day out in 1872 as they walked through what would later be known as Kelvingrove Park in Glasgow (at that time named West End Park). A discussion ensued and it was agreed they would form an Association Football Club. The game of football was sweeping the nation and the young men were fascinated.

The Rangers were born. The name itself was proposed by Moses; he liked it after seeing it in connection with Swindon Rangers, a rugby club.

It is impossible to miss the romanticism of the Rangers story, Peter McNeil was the senior of the quartet at only 17, his younger brother Moses was 16 with McBeath and Campbell both only 15 years old.

Tom Vallance was not there that day, but the 16-year-old was every bit as integral and a pivotal player in the formation and foundation of the club. Speaking at the opening of the original Ibrox Park in 1887 he said, in rather downplayed terms: 'About 15 years ago, a few lads who came from Gareloch met and endeavoured to scrape together as much as would buy a football and we went to the Glasgow Green, where we played for a year or two.'

Those 'lads from the Gareloch' would hardly believe what their dream has become.

2

Kick-Off!

Every great story needs an opening, all the goals, players, moments and trophies need to come from a single point in time. For many that is obviously the formation of the club, but just as important is that first game. The first time 'the Rangers' took to the pitch.

A modern reader wouldn't recognise the city of Glasgow in 1872 nor Britain for that matter. With industrialisation still moving at pace, slums and 6–7 day working weeks the order of the day. But there, on a crisp May day in 1872, two months after the club was formed the journey began against Callander at Flesher's Haugh on the banks of the River Clyde. The zeal for football had certainly taken off, starting a near 150-year (and counting) love affair.

Callander would go on to be swiftly dissolved in 1874 but their place in history is assured. That first game ended 0-0 with most players playing in their own everyday clothes instead of 'strips'.

Rangers' next game was a much different affair and is probably more symbolic of how they would go on to dominate the game in Scotland. Clyde (not the present club incarnation of that name) were seen off 11-0 and Rangers had their first, but not their last victory.

Two games and zero defeats. Scottish football had been put on notice.

3

The Scottish Cup

Scotland's national cup trophy stands second in prestige only to the league championship and wrapped in the romance only a historical national knockout competition can generate. First played for in 1873 between 16 clubs the trophy was first won by Queens Park Rangers. Although Queens Park would dominate the trophy's early years, they would slowly become a much smaller club and the word Rangers would make several appearances on the trophy alone.

The trophy itself stands two-feet high and predominantly cast from silver. Costing 56 pounds and 13 shillings at the time of its creation, the commission was given to Glasgow gold and silversmiths George Edward & Sons.

Although the Scottish Cup may be the second competition formed in the history of association football, the trophy itself stands as the oldest in the game. The English FA Cup is the oldest tournament, but their trophy has been replaced on more than one occasion while the Scottish Cup has remained the same since the 19th century.

Many a child has dreamt of having their club captain raise the trophy aloft. In total Rangers have won the Scottish Cup 32 times (including war years which are not classed by the club, rightly, as 'official victories').

Notable victories include the club's first-ever capture of the trophy in 1894 (defeating Celtic 3-1); the 1973 win over Celtic (again) 3-2 in what was the centenary year for Rangers and the Scottish FA, the 5-1 demolition of Hearts in 1996 (when Gordon Durie score a hat-trick but had to watch the final be dubbed 'Laudrup's game' after a sensational performance from Brian Laudrup) and who could forget the epic 3-2 victory over Celtic when Rangers came from behind twice and snatched the trophy from Martin O'Neill's men with a 90th-minute winner from striker Peter Lovenkrands.

There have also been moments of heartache as well, however, during the 20 final losses, such as the last-minute 3-2 defeat to Hibernian in 2016 (currently the last time Rangers reached the final) and the 2-1 loss to Hearts in 1998 which saw the end of the first trophy-laden Walter Smith era.

Paul Gascoine and Ally McCoist hold 1996 League Cup. *Alamy*

4

The First of Many

Ask these days and you will find there is no such trophy as the Glasgow Charity Cup (also known as the Glasgow Merchants' Charity Cup), but it holds a special place in the history of Rangers as the first official competition and piece of silverware the club won.

The tournament was created to provide a knockout format and was open to clubs from in and around the Glasgow area, although by invitation only. It consisted of only four teams playing a first round, with each winner moving into the final.

Rangers beat Third Lanark (a club no longer in existence, but at that time a successful Scottish side who won the trophy in the 1889/90 season) 4-1 in the first round before going on to meet another club no longer with us, Vale of Leven, at Hampden. Rangers won the final 2-1. Playing that day were the Vallance brothers Tom, who had played such a significant part in the club's founding and growth, and Alick who had been named as captain in 1881.

5

That First Flag

The league championship: it is the trophy all clubs aspire to and one that has helped shape and define the history of Rangers. But the first league success the club had needed to be shared with a rival.

Initial invites to join had been sent to 14 clubs: Abercorn, Cambuslang, Celtic, Cowlairs, Dumbarton, Hearts, Rangers, Renton, St Bernard's, St Mirren, Third Lanark and Vale of Leven. Clyde and Queens Park immediately declined their chance to take part.

Back in 1890, the league championship (with Rangers' William Wilton as its first treasurer) was seen as playing a secondary role behind the period's more glamourous trophies such as the Scottish Cup or Glasgow Charity Cup.

But Rangers managed to get their hands on that first-ever championship trophy, starting a near 150-year entanglement. It is fair to say that as far as the league is concerned, it, and Rangers' DNA, is mixed. Rangers were there on the ground on day one, winning titles. But on this first occasion, and maybe in a beautiful link between the old 'big' clubs and the growing power of Rangers, this league title was shared with Dumbarton.

Rangers and Dumbarton had dominated the season with the Gers suffering a solitary loss in their initial 15 games (of an 18-game season). This was neck-and-neck stuff as Rangers hosted title rivals

Dumbarton on the penultimate day knowing a win for the visitors would see them crowned champions. Rangers had other ideas, however, and goals from McCreadie, Hislop, Kerr and McPherson saw them run out 4-2 winners on the day. Next up, Celtic.

On Dumbarton's final day against St Mirren, Rangers faced the men from the East End (Rangers had a further game in hand) knowing victory would put them in the driving seat. But disaster struck as Celtic were able to conjure up a 2-1 victory whilst Dumbarton did their job of beating St Mirren.

Rangers now needed to beat Third Lanark at home or see the 'Sons of the Rock' lift the inaugural title, and in a pressure game overcame nerves to secure a 4-1 win, with Alick McKenzie the hero with a hat-trick.

A league committee meeting determined a play-off was required with Dumbarton and Rangers locked at the top on 29 points (this was before goal difference was used; had it been, Dumbarton would have edged the title). Cathkin Park was to be the venue. In the meantime, Dumbarton knocked Rangers out of the Charity Cup.

And so, to the shoot-out, winner takes all. Rangers dominated and thanks to goals from Hislop and McCreadie raced into a two-goal lead. But Dumbarton were not joint leaders for nothing and roared back into the game to make it 2-2 and end the stronger without finding a winner.

A further league committee meeting was necessary in which the vote was deadlocked until the chairman cast the decider. No more replays, the inaugural league would go to both Rangers and Dumbarton.

It may have been shared but fans can rightly claim Rangers Football Club as Kings of Scotland, right from the start.

6

Old Firm Victory #1

Saturday, 18 February 1893, four days after Valentine's. It is a day that every Rangers fan should celebrate with just as much fervour as they do the festival of love.

On that day, Rangers started a love affair with beating Celtic by recording their first-ever victory against the men from the East End of the city. Deciding to do it in a cup final really does feel just like Rangers, who throughout their history have invariably 'turned up' when needed.

Around 10,000 filed into the now disused Cathkin Park to watch the Glasgow Cup Final that day, with Celtic strong favourites (the club had been formed just five years before but had swiftly become a strong force in the game) to record their third straight cup victory.

On a waterlogged pitch Rangers started energetically, belying their position as underdogs, and thanks to clever formation and play from the likes of Neil Kerr and captain David Mitchell, subdued Celtic's formidable forward line.

A 1-0 half-time lead courtesy of Kerr was thoroughly deserved, and Rangers went 3-0 up after the break thanks to another from Kerr, and McPherson. Celtic did manage a consolation goal in the final few seconds, but the final result of 3-1 to Rangers did not flatter the victors in the slightest, who had dominated proceedings from the first whistle.

These were the days when football was a gentleman's game and reports of the time noted the goodwill of the Celtic officials in agreeing Rangers were deserved victors on the day. A far cry from blaming referees or the weather as many a modern manager does now!

7

Scottish Cup #1

1873 saw the first staging of the Scottish Cup, yet it evaded Rangers' best attempts to get hold of it for 20 years, with the club defeated twice in the final until a sodden Glasgow February day in 1894.

Celtic presented the final foe this time around in a first-ever Scottish Cup Old Firm final. They had managed to win the tournament in the 1891/92 season and after a void game (due to a frozen pitch) had narrowly lost out in the 1892/93 season in a replay 2-1 to Queens Park.

Even though Rangers had seen off the likes of Cowlairs, Leith, Clyde and Queens Park along the way (scoring 18 and only conceding one) they were still considered underdogs by the media and by the majority of the boisterous 17,000 crowd watching at Hampden Park that day.

The weather had reduced the surface to that of a field and as the players kicked off it was noticed that their boots sank into the ground in places. Celtic had the better of the early exchanges with Rangers captain David Mitchell cajoling and encouraging his men to action.

It was 0-0 at half-time, with Rangers having relied on wasteful Celtic finishing and stout defensive play from the likes of Smith and Drummond with Haddow in goal.

Rangers started the second half brightly and opened the scoring through McCreadie. Better fitness and positioning then began to tell as the Gers took control of the game with Barker adding a second before McPherson sealed the destination of the trophy. Celtic did rally slightly and got a consolation goal for their fans.

All agreed Rangers had been on top and decisively handled the league champions. More importantly, that first Scottish Cup had found its way into Light Blue hands. Only once more in their respective histories would Rangers and the trophy wait so long to embrace.

8

First Flotation

On Monday 6 March 1899 a small article appeared in the now defunct *Scottish Referee* newspaper, headed 'Proposed Flotation'. It read, amongst other things: 'Next Monday evening a meeting of the Rangers F.C officials and members will be held to consider the proposal to form the club into a limited company.'

The club was looking to raise funds to erect an 'enclosure', a stadium in modern terms, and to do so were forced to take the step of a share issue (many a modern chairman can sympathise I suspect).

So began the club's relationship with share issues and capital-led ownership which would bring great success and arguably even greater calamity. So 9,000 ordinary shares were offered at £1 per share, with another 600 propriety shares priced at £5 each, enough to perhaps pay for a feasibility report into the proposed work these days.

At this time Rangers had around 600 members in the club, and the article gave room to mention that, given the numbers, it was unlikely shares would find their way into the hands of 'outsiders'.

Rangers had already built a strong family feel to the club and outside investment was not a preferred option. Of course, the members subscribed; the blue pound has always been strong.

9

Merchants' Charity Cup Final

On 17 May 1900 the siege of British forces by South African Boers under General Conje was broken. It had lasted 217 days and the defence, led by future Boys Scouts founder Robert Baden-Powell, was stout, energetic and battle-ready.

Five days earlier and roughly 13,000 kilometres away a different sort of struggle was taking place as Rangers laid siege to Celtic's defence in the Glasgow Merchants' Charity Cup Final.

Both teams came into the game with silverware already successfully landed, Rangers had claimed the Scottish league and Glasgow Cup whilst Celtic had bagged the Scottish Cup and Inter-City League (a competition for clubs from Glasgow and Edinburgh).

The Merchants' Cup was the final trophy of the season and Celtic came in as favourites having recently beaten Rangers home and away in the Inter-City League.

But Rangers started surprisingly brightly, using pace and endeavour to fashion an opening through Smith which ended with a Celtic own goal. Rangers then settled down into their rhythm and it was no surprise when Campbell and Gibson added to make it 3-0 at half-time.

There was to be no relief for the embattled Celtic defence in the second half as Hamilton made it 4-0. A consolation goal came, but one can only imagine the Celtic players' and fans' despair as Miller scored for Rangers to seal a humiliating defeat (they even managed to miss a late penalty).

Both teams were somewhat criticised by the press for their use of the offside rules to slow down the game and not attacking as much as they should have. However, £1,027 had been raised for charitable causes which meant those in need were the true winners.

Some 15,000 had been treated to a fantastic display by Rangers who had thrashed their opponents and done what the South Africans could not, that is successfully take apart a defence.

10

Religion and Unionism

In the modern era, the club, its ethos, founding and fans have been somewhat unfairly (and lazily) branded as being steeped in a historical aura of 'Protestants only'. To add even more Clydeside mud to the water, this laziness extended to Celtic, who were given the mantle of being the 'Catholic' club based on their historical links to the Church and Irish diaspora.

There is no question that Rangers as a club have always had a strong link to the ethos of a United Kingdom and attracted as supporters people who supported the Union, including those from Northern Ireland. However, it was a later ideology which meant that Catholic players were not seen as the right fit for the blue jersey, although the club and fanbase have now shaken this off to become a vibrant and diverse community fit for all.

The ideological birth of Rangers was not intended to promote any political, social or religious beliefs or identity whatsoever. When Peter and Moses McNeil, Peter Campbell and William McBeath walked through West End Park in Glasgow (now enlarged and re-named Kelvingrove Park) their sole focus was in creating a club to further their friendship and their passion for association football and maybe, just maybe, win some fans and trophies along the way.

In those latter two attempts those boys, and those who came after, certainly succeeded. The world's most successful football team and a religion to its loyal fan base all on its own.

11

The 'Old Firm'

A term known globally and a brand co-owned by both Rangers and Celtic, the term 'Old Firm' is shorthand for one of the game's great and lasting rivalries.

Rangers are the more senior club, having come into existence 14 years before their rival from Glasgow's East End. They have also won more trophies during their respective histories.

Two passionate tribes sharing one city, sometimes green but more often than not blue, but when did both clubs become known collectively?

The term actually originated in the early years of the 1900's and was a caustic take by naysayers on the monies which seemed to pour into each club, in part from their regular meetings. A familiar strain of people envying big clubs. And Celtic.

It was in fact such a view, from both sets of supporters, that saw them join in a combined riot after the 1909 Scottish Cup Final when it became clear that the replay, having ended 1-1 (after a 2-2 draw in the first game) would require yet another replay to be played to decide the result, instead of extra time. Disgruntled fans caused havoc for three hours, in the process injuring over 130 people and leading to £150 fines for each club and a withholding of the trophy by the Scottish Football Association.

These days the term is used jointly by the clubs to promote their 'brand' in the ever merchandise and financially savvy modern game.

12

The Draw's the Thing

2-2 is a draw right? Seems sensible, so how could a 2-2 draw result in Rangers winning a cup final (without extra time or penalties)?

October 1901: Rangers and Celtic face off in the 14th iteration of the Glasgow Cup Final at Ibrox on a beautifully sunny day as 38,000 waited patiently for Glasgow's big two to fight to the finish.

Celtic started well but were stunned when Rangers engineered a two-goal lead within the first 15 minutes through Speedie and Wilkie. Celtic roared back into life and with the help of a penalty managed to get themselves back level.

The game ebbed and flowed but as the final whistle blew both teams were locked at 2-2 so a replay was the agreed order of the day. And so, to that Rangers win . . .

After the match both teams retired to the Alexandra Hotel in Bath Street Glasgow for drinks and socialising at which both clubs' officials set out to agree the replay venue. This was where disagreement started, with the Celtic officials demanding Parkhead be the venue whilst the Rangers officials remained steadfast in their choice of Ibrox.

Celtic made a dubious claim that a Rangers director had agreed that in the event of a draw the game would go to Parkhead; this was never acknowledged by Rangers. For their part Rangers believed precedent favoured them with previous replays being held at the same venue. To add more complexity the Glasgow Football Association (who held an interest in the gate money) were against the proposed use of the Glasgow Exhibition Ground on the basis it would affect gate receipts. Finally, the association broke the deadlock, precedent would stand, and the game would be played at Ibrox.

Celtic reacted to the news badly and immediately tendered their resignation from the competition (interestingly Rangers had done likewise in 1879 but this was due to being injury-ravaged and unable to field a team, having had a request to move the date refused).

Rangers offered to play the game at a neutral ground to defuse the situation and give the supporters a chance to watch the final but Celtic would not be brought back to the table. A week passed with nothing from Celtic by way of communication, so the Association awarded the trophy and honour to Rangers.

13

Toffee Bob

With over 1,000 locations across the UK, chances are you may have stopped in at a 'McColls' newsagent at some point. Older readers may recall when it was RS McColls before the corporate rebranding dropped the initials.

The link to Rangers? In between becoming a mainstay on the high street, the eponymous Robert Smyth McColl was also a classy, if unsuccessful, player for the club.

He opened his confectionery shop in 1901 with his brother Tom and was soon blessed with the nickname 'Toffee Bob'. In 1904 Rangers manager William Wilton paid Newcastle United £300 to bring him north of the border.

Unfortunately, he was unable to win any trophies during his time at Rangers despite a healthy one goal in two ratio. He was also prolific at international level, scoring 13 times in 13 games for Scotland, including a hat-trick in a 4-1 win over England.

He ended his time at Queens Park, signing off his career by scoring six goals in his last game before concentrating on his businesses.

14

Arsenal Shares

Many clubs have longstanding relationships with each other; sometimes these are due to geography, shared players or rivalries. So, what linked Scotland's top side with one of the most famous London clubs – Arsenal FC?

In 1910 Arsenal (Woolwich Arsenal as they were known then) were in a perilous financial state and facing potential liquidation. With no readily available funds they offered a share issue to investors. With shares costing the princely sum of £1 (an Arsenal share of today would cost you tens of thousands), it failed to deliver the desired take-up.

Then Arsenal manager George Morrell had a familiarity and friendship with Rangers' manager William Wilton and wrote to him seeking any aid that could be forthcoming. Rangers ultimately purchased two shares and had a direct hand in keeping one of English football's leading clubs in business.

The closeness between both clubs grew more personal with the great friendship between legendary managers Bill Struth and Arsenal's Herbert Chapman, so much so that Chapman had a direct hand in Arsenal's decision to gift Rangers a further 14 shares in the 1930s as a thank you for their support during the club's darkest moments. Rangers had also beaten Arsenal in this period (1933) in a 'battle of champions' which pitted the respective league holders of Scotland and England against each other, with Rangers winning 2-0 at home and 3-1 away.

In May 2011 Scottish venture capitalist Craig Whyte purchased the controlling interest in the club from David Murray. In May 2012 it was reported and subsequently confirmed that Whyte had decided to forgo 102 years of shared history and had sold the shares to Uzbek-Russian businessman Alisher Usmanov for circa £230,000 in the midst of Rangers' financial woes. Fans were horrified to learn that, on top of this, Whyte had demanded the proceeds were transferred not to the club's bank account but his own.

Bill Struth and Herbert Chapman on the 1st tee at Turnberry Golf Club, September 1933, when Arsenal came north to play Rangers at Ibrox.

15

Postbox – Walter Tull

In September 2020, Royal Mail produced a set of black postboxes across the UK to highlight the lives of significant members of the black British community. One such celebrated the life and tragic death of Walter Tull.

Born in Folkestone, Kent on 28 April 1888 to an English mother and Barbadian father, Tull was a professional footballer for Northampton and Tottenham Hotspur who fought to defend Britain in the First World War at battles such as the Somme and Passchendaele.

When the First World War was declared in 1914, Walter was the first Northampton footballer to join the army, enrolling with the Football Battalion (17th Middlesex Regiment).

On his return to the UK in 1916 he enrolled in officer training (having been promoted to sergeant during his initial service). Due to racial prejudices of the time he needed to gain special dispensation as only white officers were allowed. This was given and led to him going on to become the first black officer to command regular British troops.

Having signed for Rangers (in the process becoming the club's first black player) he was tragically destined to never pull on the famous blue jersey. In March 1918, just four months after signing for the club he was killed in the line of duty whilst leading his men. Despite the efforts of his unit, heavy machine-gun fire

meant his body could not be recovered.

A man who broke barriers and prejudices through integrity and duty, sadly lost before he could bring those virtues to Rangers.

16

Captains of History

In total, 32 men have had the honour of wearing the captain's armband since the club's creation in March 1872.

*Name	Period Active	Nation
Tom Vallance (first known captain)	1876–1882	Scotland
David Mitchell	1882–1894	Scotland
John McPherson	1894–1898	Scotland
Robert Hamilton	1898–1906	Scotland
Robert Campbell	1906–1916	Scotland
Tommy Cairns	1916–1926	Scotland
Bert Manderson	1926–1927	England
Tommy Muirhead	1927–1930	Scotland
David Meiklejon	1930–1938	Scotland
Jimmy Simpson	1938–1940	Scotland
Jock Shaw	1940–1953	Scotland
George Young	1953–1957	Scotland
Ian McColl	1957–1960	Scotland
Eric Caldow	1960–1962	Scotland
Bobby Shearer	1962–1965	Scotland
John Greig	1965–1978	Scotland
Derek Johnstone	1978–1983	Scotland

John McClelland	1983–1984	Scotland
Craig Paterson	1984–1986	Scotland
Terry Butcher	1986–1990	England
Richard Gough	1990–1997	Scotland
	1997–1998	
Lorenzo Amoruso	1998–2000	Italy
Barry Ferguson	2000–2003	Scotland
	2005–2007	
	2007–2009	
Craig Moore	2003–2004	Australia
Stefan Klos	2004–2005	Germany
Gavin Rae	2007	Scotland
David Weir	2009–2012	Scotland
Steven Davis	2012	Northern Ireland
Carols Bocanegra	2012	USA
Lee McCulloch	2015–	Scotland
Lee Wallace	2015–2018	Scotland
James Tavernier	2018–	England

*List excludes one-game captains

17

Tragedy on the Water

To lose a dear friend to a tragic accident is hard to bear; that friend being at the height of their ability and powers only adds to the tragedy.

William Wilton had just managed Rangers to the championship title (in the process taking it back from Celtic and playing lauded football, scoring 106 goals and conceding only 25) and so was in high spirits when he embarked on a day out on the water on 2 May 1920. It would become a dark day in the history of the club as Wilton was swept to his death from the deck of his friend James Marr's yacht.

He had been a colossal force within the club and his impact on helping to make it pre-eminent in the Scottish game cannot be overstated.

His story is entwined with Rangers like few others. Attached to the club for 16 years in administrative capacities, such as match secretary (also playing for the reserve side the 'Rangers Swifts'), he was also a committee member, which included being one of the principal founders of the league before becoming the club's first 'official' manager, in today's understanding, in 1899.

He also instituted the Rangers fund to raise money for those affected by the 1902 Ibrox Park disaster (following a Scotland v England match), raising £4,000 in the process.

In the ten years he held the post of match secretary, Rangers won two Scottish championships (1890/91 and 1898/99) as well as three Scottish Cups (1894, 1897 and 1898). This included a 100 per cent record league season (1898/99) when Rangers set a world record which stands to this day. No other team has gone through their domestic season winning all games. Rangers' record stands at 18 played, 18 won with 79 goals scored.

Under his guidance as manager a further seven more league championships would be won (some with the legendary Bill Struth as his assistant).

Reporting on his death, an article in the *Glasgow Herald* stated, 'Mr Wilton brought the qualities that were required to maintain the high standing of the club and its very successful career is a tribute to the way in which he guided its affairs.'

Wilton provided success on the pitch, the framework and standards required of a Ranger off it and helped set the foundations for the club to dominate until the outbreak of the Second World War.

Final word goes to then Rangers President Sir John Ure Primrose who described Wilton as a 'prince among managers' who 'strove to keep the game of football free from blemish', adding that 'the club which he managed is one of the most popular in the United Kingdom and its record during Mr Wilton's management reflects the attention and influence he exercised over it'.

18

The Medals Won by Mr Bob McPhail

Many players are never lucky enough to win anything in their careers so imagine having a career than ends with you needing a cabinet just for your medals!

One of seven brothers (his brother Malcolm managed a Scottish Cup win with Kilmarnock), McPhail was part of the Rangers team that dominated the 1920s after joining from Airdrie (where he won his first Scottish medal in 1924, playing with the likes of 'Wembley Wizard' Hughie Gallacher, beating Hibs 2-0 in the last final to be played at Ibrox until the 1997 iteration).

A humorous and humble man, Bob hadn't even bothered recording his goals scored for Rangers until he was told his long-held record was being threatened. The new kid on the block was one A McCoist, not a bad replacement all things told (Bob's tally of 230 league goals makes him Rangers' highest goalscorer of the pre-Second World War era with McCoist the only player ahead of him overall).

Also, a proud international, his first appearance for Scotland against England at Hampden in 1927 didn't end so well. This was a different time, but even he was surprised to discover the older Scottish players taking to the port and brandy before the game's start, persuading the 22-year-old McPhail to partake.

A torrid first 45 minutes ensued. At half-time, Rangers manager Bill Struth strode into the Scotland dressing room and, after working out the cause of McPhail's poor performance, forced him to be sick before resuming play. Lesson learned you might say.

But on the domestic front McPhail was making defenders feel light-headed, having a particularly fruitful relationship with 'The Wee Blue Devil' Alan Morton.

All in, Bob's medal collection still stands as one of the finest in Scottish football. In total his record over 12 years at the club stands at nine League championships, six Scottish Cups, six Charity Cups and five Glasgow Cups.

Bob McPahil (left).

19

The Keys to the City

Cracking America: it has been a dream of performers and artists since the rediscovery of the continent.

Rangers can claim to have done that to some degree in 1928. Having secured the 1927/28 season league championship, manager Bill Struth took his squad on a club first-ever tour of the United States (Canada also briefly featured).

The six-week tour saw Rangers play ten matches in all, staying undefeated with seven wins and three draws.

The opening game saw the all-conquering champions defeat Eastern Pennsylvania 8-2 in treacherous weather conditions. A 0-0 draw with American champions Fall River Marksmen followed (with reports of the time suggesting Rangers were lucky to escape defeat).

Following a few days' rest, Rangers returned to action on 9 June against the Western Pennsylvania All-Stars in Pittsburgh. In another torrential downpour they rediscovered their form and trounced the Americans 9-0.

After the match the then mayor of Pittsburgh, the Republican Charles H Kline (who would go on to be both convicted and then acquitted on 49 counts of corruption) presented Struth, the players and club officials with a handsome gold key to the city.

20

The 50th Scottish Cup

Over 118,000 fans packed into Hampden Stadium to watch Rangers and Celtic contest the 50th Scottish Cup Final in April 1928.

Rangers' estrangement from the trophy for a quarter of a century had become something of a go-to joke for performers and rival fans but there was hope among the blue legions and, importantly, in the Rangers dressing room too!

Celtic came in as strong favourites to lift the trophy and started with intent, testing Rangers keeper Hamilton several times but without success. A nervous first half for the Gers fans, but they could breathe a sigh of relief as the players headed in for half-time at 0-0. The cup was still up for grabs.

Fiery words may have been spoken in the Rangers camp during the break because they returned for the second half with renewed verve and vigour, taking the game to Celtic across the entire pitch. Referee Willie Bell then entered proceedings when he correctly adjudged handball in the Celtic box against Willie McStay and awarded a penalty to Rangers.

Captain Meiklejohn did what all Rangers captains should do and shouldered the responsibility. With a steely eye and a calm demeanour, he smashed the ball into the back of the net to give Rangers an important lead.

Within 12 minutes all Celtic resistance had crumbled as Rangers stretched into a 3-0 lead thanks to a goal from the legendary Bob McPhail and a third from Sandy Archibald. He would add a fourth soon after.

The long wait was over, and Rangers had finally reclaimed the Scottish Cup, congratulations were received from around the globe from the Rangers community and the players celebrated over dinner and drinks in Glasgow surrounded by red-white-and-blue flags mixed with Union Jacks.

That opening goal was decisive in setting Rangers on their way to bringing the Scottish Cup home, so captain Meiklejohn has the last word: 'I am too pleased to be able to express my true feelings . . . I have never felt so anxious in my life. I can tell you I was glad when I saw the ball in the back of the net.'

Action from the 1928 Scottish Cup Final.

21

Home

In the archives of Glasgow's Mitchell Library, you will find a series of drawings by the architect Archibald Leitch. These document the building and rebuilding of the place Rangers now call home, Ibrox Stadium.

But it took Rangers some time to arrive at the site fans now know. At their formation in 1872 Rangers played their games at Flesher's Haugh on the banks of the River Clyde.

The 1875/76 season saw them playing at Burnbank and subsequently Kinning Park, where the site of the first Ibrox is unfortunately now roadway.

In 1899 the site of the current stadium was opened. Designed by Leitch, it housed an oval track around the pitch, with a pavilion and one stand. The terracing was formed by wooden planks bolted on to a framework made of iron. A similar wooden terracing was constructed at the eastern end.

At a Scotland v England match on 5 April 1902, disaster struck when the terracing collapsed. A subsequent inquiry found problems with the wood used, weaker yellow instead of red pine. Both the supplier and Leitch were interviewed but no charges were made. Leitch was so worried by the event's impact on his business that he wrote to the club begging to be given the chance to design the revamped stadium.

The club agreed and he embarked on ensuring this new version would be safer than any before. But his enduring legacy is the sweeping Welsh brick façade with its towering windows, arguably the most beautiful face to a stadium anywhere in the world and a listed building in Scotland (meaning it cannot be materially tampered with) opened in 1929.

Since then, Glasgow has changed beyond recognition, and the stadium itself has seen expansion and modernisation; however, the club has endured and on Edmiston Drive every brick, rivet and bolt bears its weight of history, standing in muted respect to those who have gone before and the unimpeachable majesty of Rangers Football Club.

Rangers play Motherwell at Ibrox Park in 1920. The pavilion and grandstand that can be seen on the right of the pitch were replaced by the Bill Struth Stand in 1928. The 'Bovril Stand' (North Stand) can be seen on the left.

22

The Tragedy of Sam English & John Thomson

'They realise it was an accident, pure and simple.' So read a simple line in a public notice in the Tuesday, 8 September 1931 edition of the Dundee *Evening Telegraph & Post*. That notice had been requested by the family of Celtic goalkeeper John Thomson who had tragically died due to injuries sustained in a clash with Rangers' Sam English during an Old Firm game three days earlier.

They went on to make clear they completely exonerated English for any blame. He was, however, unable to exonerate himself.

Ulsterman English was first and foremost a phenomenal goal-scorer, as his 44 goals for Rangers in the 1931/32 season attest to. In a tragic twist, English had not originally been scheduled to play against Celtic in that early season Old Firm match due to an ankle knock sustained against Falkirk, but his replacement Jimmy Smith was laid low with a cold on matchday.

The game itself was uneventful from a football perspective, the 80,000 crowd treated to more wrestling between players than actual play. Into the second half and a neat through ball sent English surging into the box.

Thomson, known as a brave goalkeeper, raced from his line and dived at English's feet, getting a touch on the ball and saving a surely certain goal. On the carry through, however, his head collided with English's leg leaving him unconscious and medical staff immediately called. Thomson would fail to recover and would pass away. A sad moment for all fans and one which cast a cloud over English that would never lift.

Despite the Thomson family's expressed support for English, some Celtic fans could not forget and hounded the Rangers man, to the extent that, even after he left Rangers for Liverpool in 1933 to attempt a fresh start, they would travel south to remind him.

English never fully recovered from the tragedy and the resulting focus on it as his defining moment. His family later paid for the Sam English Bowl to be produced, a silver bowl holding 44 silver balls (representing each of his goals in that 1931/32 season) which is presented to Rangers' top scorer each season.

A tragic moment that united Scottish football in sorrow.

23

Willie Thornton

Thornton, aided by his great friend Willie Waddell, was devastating in front of goal with a keen intelligence of the game, and it was no surprise he became the first post-war Ranger to break the 100-goal barrier on his way to racking up 188 goals in 303 games.

Often referred to as 'old-fashioned' due to his style of centre-forward play and his gentlemanly conduct he is rightly a Rangers hall-of-famer.

He joined the Gers at 16 years old from Winchburg Albion in March 1936 on £1 per week, making his debut against Partick Thistle in January 1937. He signed professional forms a few months later before forcing his way into a regular starting position in the side for the 1938/39 campaign which brought him the first of his four championship medals.

The Second World War interrupted with Willie serving in the British Army's only private regiment, the Duke of Atholl's Scottish Horse. He served with great honour and distinction, being awarded the Military Medal for his gallant service in the Sicilian campaign.

When football and normality finally returned so too did the Thornton goal threat. In the 1947/48 Scottish Cup semi-final against Hibernian a record 143,570 people saw the tie won thanks to a Thornton header from a terrific Waddell cross. Of course, Rangers went on to win the final too.

In 1952 he was voted Scotland's Player of the Year but decided to retire just two years later, moving into management with Dundee and then Partick Thistle, before returning to Ibrox as assistant manager to Davie White.

When Waddell replaced the unfortunate White, there was no chance he would remove his old friend and the double act which had been so successful for Rangers on the field was replicated off it, culminating in a dream night in Spain. However, Thornton was asked to take control of Rangers for two games in this period and recorded two wins, a clear 100 per cent record!

He sadly passed in August 1991 but left behind his post-war record as well as four league championships, three Scottish Cups and three League Cups. Not to mention an impeccable reputation and the happy memories he helped create.

24

The Loving Cup

Tradition: sometimes it is an anchor in a storm, a phrase, a way of doing things that reminds us of who we are and what we stand for. Traditions also help to bind people to a common cause, such as the defence of the realm and the defence of one's club.

So it is that Rangers have the Loving Cup ceremony each New Year's Day (or nearest home fixture) with visiting club directors to toast the monarch's health. But the cup itself came into Rangers' possession in tragic circumstances.

Thirty identical cups were cast from the same mould (which was subsequently destroyed) in May 1937 to celebrate the coronation of their majesties King George VI and Queen Elizabeth (the current Queen's mother). These were gifted to all 22 clubs in the then English First Division with others going to the likes of the British Museum and the King himself. The cup is three-handled, each in the style of a knot, and on the cup is an inscription testifying to its purpose as well as the royal coat of arms.

Tragedy struck in the July of that year at the Brymbo colliery in Staffordshire, close to Stoke-on-Trent where the cups had been made. Explosions, fire and smoke inhalation had killed 31 miners and injured several more.

Rangers were even at that time a household name and were asked to take part in a benefit match to raise funds for the victims' families. Bill Struth immediately accepted and prepared to lead his men south.

On 19 October, Rangers played out a 0-0 draw with Stoke City in front of a huge crowd with all monies going to the charitable fund. Afterwards Stoke City President, Sir Francis Joseph gifted his own club's cup to Rangers as a thank you, with one caveat. That it be used to toast the monarch's health each year.

Traditions are our history and each incumbent of the Rangers manager's and directors' offices have upheld this one.

Stoke City President, Sir Francis Joseph, presents the Loving Cup to Rangers in 1937.

25

Waddell

Most journalists talk a good game, but when it comes to playing or managing at the highest level their opinions are as empty as their non-existent trophy cabinets. Not so player, manager, administrator and journalist Willie Waddell.

A dashing right-winger, he made his first senior appearance for Rangers as a 17-year-old in a 1938 friendly against Arsenal, scoring the winning goal. His pay of £2 a week arguably the best bit of business Bill Struth ever concluded, particularly when Portsmouth had offered him £6 a week.

Like most players of the time his career was cut short by the intervention of the Second World War. However, he was still able to claim not only widespread praise but also four league championships, two Scottish Cups and a host of inter-war year trophies before retiring in 1955.

He moved into journalism with the now defunct newspaper the Glasgow *Evening Citizen*, becoming a must-read columnist. However, within a year he would take up the manager's role at Kilmarnock. He would be there for eight seasons, in the process turning the small club into Scottish champions in his final season (1964/65), winning the title from Hearts at Tynecastle on the final day through goal difference.

He resigned and returned to journalism, becoming respected thanks to his open and fair analysis at the Scottish *Daily Express*, including watching as Jock Stein's Celtic effected a stranglehold on the Scottish game. He even predicted Celtic's European Cup triumph, confidently declaring they would bring the trophy home for Britain.

It was almost inevitable when David White was sacked that Waddell's name would enter the conversation for who would become Rangers' manager. In his final column he confirmed he would be taking up the position, giving an insight into why he had turned away the likes of Manchester City and Wolves, signing off with 'once a Rangers, always a Ranger'.

The Waddell years had begun.

He uplifted the standards and discipline across the club immediately, recalling the Struthian era. No one was spared and everyone knew who was boss.

The 16-year-old Derek Johnstone famously rose to place a header beyond a despairing Celtic goalkeeper to give Waddell his first trophy, the League Cup in 1970/71 season. For Rangers and Waddell, the best was yet to come.

Season 1971/72 would end in immortality for the squad and vindication for Waddell. Unable to win the league championship he would deliver Rangers' first, and to date only, European trophy on a breathless night in Barcelona, defeating Dynamo Moscow 3-2.

However, as the Rangers fans sobered up and began to dream of what could be, Waddell dropped the bombshell that he was being replaced as manager by Jock Wallace and he would become general manager of the club instead.

Rangers would win the league twice in the next four seasons as Waddell took on UEFA over a two-year European ban on the club following disturbances after the final. He was unable to overturn the ban completely, but had it reduced to one year, advising fans afterwards that pitch invasions wouldn't be tolerated by the club ever again.

Willie Waddell in 1975.

Arguably his finest moment was born out of tragedy, following the Ibrox disaster of 1972, when he took a leading role in the rebuilding of Ibrox Stadium, determining it be upgraded completely with supporter safety as the primary concern.

Managing director when Rangers ended Celtic's attempt for a tenth successive title, he stepped down from all duties in 1979 after a 40-year relationship with the club. A giant in the history of the club who delivered their greatest single night he, for a long time, was Rangers, handing them back a pride and standing which had been lost.

How Can You Buy Willie Waddell?

You will read more on Willie Waddell the player, manager and journalist in this volume; however, below is a poem that was sung by Rangers fans when there was talk of him being transferred during his playing days under Bill Struth:

An Englishman Landed In Edmiston Drive And Watched Willie Waddell With Critical Eye
'How Can I Buy Him?' He Asked Mr Struth
And Bill He Replied, 'I'll Tell You The Truth.'

Chorus
How Can You Buy All The Cups That We've Won And How Can You Buy Mrs Thorton's Son? How Can You Buy Our Big Geordie Young? And How Can You Buy Willie Waddell? Nature Bestowed All Her Gifts With A Smile, The Right Foot, The Left Foot, The 'Noddle'. When You Can Buy All These Wonderful Things Then You Can Buy Willie Waddell

Verse
'I'll Give Thirty Thousand,' The Englishman Said, 'And Also A Star,' Mr Struth Shook His Head. 'You Can Give Thirty Thousand, Stars, Moon And Sun But You Still Can't Have Waddell, There's Only One.'

Waddell would never be sold nor play for another club after being a Ranger.

Willie Waddell in action in 1929.

27

The Bruce

Robert I, known as Robert the Bruce, was the King of the Scots who fought a successful campaign against the English crown.

He died on 7 June 1329 a mere 543 years before the founding of Rangers, so what is his link to the Ibrox trophy room?

Upon his death he asked for his heart to be taken to the Holy Land and used to inspire Christians in their fight against the Muslim populace of the region. An ornate silver casket was made to carry the heart, but it only made it to Spain before being returned after several of the accompanying Scottish nobles were killed in battle against the Moors.

Fast forward to the summer of 1941 in the midst of the Second World War, when then Glasgow Lord Provost Sir Patrick Dollan asked if Rangers would be kind enough to play England's Preston North End to raise money for the Glasgow War Fund.

Ever the charitable club, of course Rangers accepted and played out a 3-1 victory at Ibrox in September of that year. Sir Patrick wished to mark the game with a winner's trophy of sorts and decided upon a replica of the King's casket (known as the Bruce Casket) which Rangers duly took into their possession where it has been ever since.

Rangers: Dawson, Shaw, Gray, Little, Woodburn, Symon, McIntosh, Gillick, Venters, Smith, Beattie

28

Eight Going on Eighteen

Celtic have their 'Hampden in the sun' 7-1 moment. So, let's talk about New Year's Day 1943, when Celtic scored one but Rangers were Gr-eight!

Still an Old Firm record score, Rangers dominated in this game even prior to Celtic having two men dismissed (the score was already a very healthy 4-1 to the Gers before that happened).

Rangers had set the intent (and destination of the points) early, scoring twice in the game's opening four minutes. Celtic got one back and going in at half-time only one behind believed they could get back into the game.

An equaliser for Celtic was judged offside and this spurred Rangers into action. Goal number three swiftly followed before a fourth was registered after an ill-dealt-with ball into the Celtic box ended with a deflected Waddell goal. That fourth goal led Celtic's Malcolm McDonald to question the competence of the referee's decision, believing Waddell was offside; he was immediately ordered off the field.

The Celtic players did not take this well and several minutes passed before the game could be restarted. However, no sooner had the game begun than Celtic were down to nine men after full-back Matt Lynch gave what would be described as 'dissent' to the referee following a disputed free-kick decision. Waddell added a fifth, Young a sixth from the penalty spot before Gillick (who had suffered a serious head knock but refused to leave the field) scored twice to get his hat-trick.

8-1; this time Rangers were in the sun and a large portion of the 30,000 attendance went home very happy.

Rangers; Dawson, Gray, Shaw, Little, Young, Symon, Waddell, Duncanson, Gillick, Venters, Johnstone

Celtic: Miller, Dornan, Lynch, M McDonald, Paterson, Corbett, Delaney, McAuley, Airlie, McGowan, Duncan

29

Post-War Victory

The Second World War had wracked the globe, but particularly Europe with conflict and destruction.

Although football had continued throughout the war years on a non-professional basis, it had rightly taken a backseat to the carnage and horror being played out across the continent and in bombing raids up and down what Churchill had described as 'this island nation'.

But with eventual success over the Nazi threat came a renewed effort to return the country to normality, to celebrate and enjoy those things that had been mainstays of life before the shadow of conflict had fallen across the UK.

As such it was decided in 1946 to celebrate the end of hostilities by having teams play for a new one-off trophy, the 'Victory Cup' or 'War Challenge Cup'. Given the calendar precluded the Scottish Cup being held as a competition this swiftly became the sought-after trophy for clubs.

The trophy itself, played between May and June, saw Rangers play teams across two legs (this was the first round only with all succeeding rounds being one-off knockout ties). First up was Stenhousemuir, who were dispatched 8-2 on aggregate (two 4-1 victories).

In the second round Airdrieonians were the challenge in an away tie that finished 4-0 to the Gers in the process providing the light blues with revenge for having been defeated in a similar 1919 iteration of the competition.

The quarter-final saw Rangers drawn against Falkirk with the tie finishing 1-1. A replay was soon scheduled with Rangers overcoming the 'Bairns' 2-0 to set up a semi-final trip to Hampden, the national stadium.

Historical foes Celtic stood in the way of a final appearance and in front of a boisterous crowd of over 90,000 played out a 0-0 draw. No shoot-outs, back to another replay four days after the first game, this time rampant Rangers won 2-0 with Celtic having two men sent off.

The final against Hibernian was a showpiece given extra spice in the Shaw household as brothers Jock (Hibs) and Davie (Rangers) lined up against each other.

It would be Davie celebrating, along with the majority of the over 100,000 crowd as the men from the capital were sent back to the east coast empty-handed. Goals from Gillick and Duncanson (two) saw Rangers, under manager Bill Struth, add another trophy to the history of the club.

Churchill

Arguably the greatest British statesman of them all, and certainly the greatest wartime leader, Sir Winston Leonard Spencer Churchill visited Ibrox on 26 May 1949 with his wife Clementine Ogilvy Hozier (known as Clemmie).

Speaking to a packed Ibrox in glorious sunshine, Sir Winston (then leader of the Conservative and Unionist Party) and Clemmie addressed the Scottish Unionist Conference.

A mere five years since the end of the Second World War, Churchill had been beaten at the 1949 General Election by Labour, under Clement Attlee (who had also served as Churchill's deputy in the wartime coalition government).

Rangers (and their supporters) had become synonymous with supporting the crown and Union, an assumption which largely persists to this day, as does the supposition that the fanbase of their main rivals Celtic, are primarily pro-Irish republican supporters.

A crowd of roughly 22,000 packed into Ibrox to hear the speakers, at that time the largest gathering of Scottish Tories on record. Sir Winston would go on to briefly serve as Prime Minister again in 1951.

In the Ibrox trophy room you will find a treasured item. A beautiful ink stand made of onyx. This was a gift from Sir Winston to the club as a thank you for hosting the occasion and in some way helping to preserve the Union against Scottish nationalism.

31

The Portrait – Bill Struth

Success: the pure, unrefined joy of the chase, relentlessly outpacing your rivals whilst, in Bill Struth's case, amassing 18 league championships, ten Scottish Cups and two League Cups in the process.

But what comes after, when your time draws to a close and you are no longer the irresistible force you once were? Apprehension, sadness and maybe even grief.

Such emotions are writ large on the portrait of Bill Struth painted by artist Charles Chapman and presented to him in May 1953 by Glasgow's Lord Provost Thomas Kerr at a gala dinner attended by Glasgow luminaries and even arch-rivals such as Celtic's Willie Maley.

An imposing piece of art, with its large carved gilded frame but small in comparison to the stature of its subject.

There he sits, in Ibrox's Blue Room, wearing one of his famous 'number one' made-to-measure blue suits. At the time of painting, his club record managerial reign of 34 years was drawing to a close with Rangers suffering some on-field turbulence including a 2-1 home defeat to East Fife, which fuelled fan protests and criticism.

Struth had arrived at Rangers in 1914 and worked as a trainer, coach and physio before being named manager. The bar was set early, when he informed the local press on his first day in the manager's office that they should never use any photographs of him in anything other than a suit as that was the dress standard of a Rangers manager. He would also go on to give service to the club as a director.

He was the man who set the standards which still exist at the club. The pre-eminence of it, from unrivalled success on the field to conduct off it. Whilst in the process of trying to sign Tommy Orr from Greenock Morton, Struth got wind that Orr's agent wanted a cut of the transfer fee and had him swiftly removed from proceedings.

But after rise comes inevitable decline. The on-field issues had led to him having already officially asked the board to bring in someone to replace him (a request initially declined but granted at the second time of asking). Struth was also suffering physically, gangrene having mandated a partial leg amputation. Less than 12 months after the portrait was handed over, the name Bill Struth would be replaced on the manager's office door.

Having instilled a culture of timeless success, the painting captures a moment of transition from the Struth era and the apprehension and sadness that must have brought him.

In a sport where the iconography of success can be easily and increasingly cheaply produced, this portrait shows the genuine article and it rightly takes pride of place in the Ibrox trophy room, surrounded by the club's league title flags.

He sadly passed in 1956 but was still a revered figure. Celtic manger James McGrory speaking at the time said, 'Mr Struth was to Rangers what Willie Maley was to Celtic for so many years. He was one of the greatest figures in the game and the Celtic officials, the players and the supporters will all be distressed by this news.'

Some people by their deeds and bearing transcend rivalry.

32

Worst Offenders

Red cards are part and parcel of the game but what happens when things get more serious? Rangers have had their fair share of questionable refereeing decisions in their history, but a prison sentence and a life ban seem over the top . . .

The three-year ban was handed out to legendary defender Willie Woodburn who signed for Rangers in October 1937. He played in Rangers' famous 'Iron Curtain' defence of the late 1940s and early 1950s along with Bobby Brown, George Young, Jock Shaw, Ian McColl and Sammy Cox, helping the club to four Scottish league championships, four Scottish Cups and two League Cups.

But Woodburn's career was prematurely ended in 1954 when he was banned *sine die* (for life) from football by the SFA following the fourth sending-off of his career.

The SFA subsequently lifted the ban after three years, but Woodburn did not return to the game.

The prison sentence belongs to striker Duncan Ferguson, who Rangers had signed from Dundee United for £4m in 1994. He became the first and only professional player in Britain to be jailed for an on-field offence after he headbutted Raith Rovers defender John McStay during a match at Ibrox that year.

Convicted of assault at Glasgow Sheriff Court he was sentenced to three months in jail, eventually serving 44 days at the city's notorious Barlinnie prison.

33

The Penalty King

Sir Alex Ferguson has seen his fair share of magnificent goals in his long and illustrious career but the best he has ever seen? That title goes to a goal scored by South African and Ranger Johnny Hubbard in a Rangers rout of Celtic in 1955.

Dubbed the 'Penalty King' due to his incredible record of 54 successful spot-kicks from 57 the South African moved to Scotland in 1949.

That goal, when Hubbard picked up the ball nearly 50 yards away from the Celtic net and beat several players including Jock Stein before rounding the goalkeeper, stopping the ball on the goal line and nonchalantly rolling it over, must have been a sight to gladden a Gers fan's heart. It is a pity no recording exists, but it did prompt one newspaper of the time to declare that 1 January, when Rangers defeated Celtic 4-1, would be called 'Hubbard day'.

Rangers hall of famer Hubbard scored a hat-trick that day, including one from the spot to add to Simpson's opener and he remains the last Rangers player to score an Old Firm league hat-trick. Celtic were brushed aside in front of a 65,000 crowd who couldn't help but appreciate the wizardry and finesse of Hubbard's play for Rangers fans it was a highlight in a season where the team struggled and finished third in the league.

Hubbard's penalty record still stands and began on 24 May 1954, on the club's Canadian Tour. His conversion streak was broken on 28 January 1956 at Broomfield Park when David Walker, the Airdrieonians goalkeeper, saved his kick, although Rangers ran out 4-0 winners. Later that year, on 22 December at Rugby Park, Kilmarnock's Jimmy Brown was the goalkeeping hero as Rangers were on the end of a 3-2 defeat.

Hubbard only missed once from the spot at Ibrox, on 16 March 1957, against Falkirk, when a save from goalkeeper Bert Slater blighted his home record, the match ending 1-1.

Johnny was a true gentleman to the last and sadly passed away in 2018.

34

Cycle of Success

Is that a bike? To anyone who has been in or seen pictures of the Ibrox trophy room that question makes sense immediately.

Underneath the stern gaze of the Bill Struth portrait stands a full-sized racing cycle. Not exactly the type of thing you would expect to find in a temple to football success you'd agree. So, who gives a bike to a club? French side Saint Étienne that's who.

Well, it isn't actually so clear-cut as there is some confusion around who provided the gift and when. Popular consensus agrees that the bike was gifted to the club by French side Saint Étienne in either 1957 or possibly 1975 prior to games and to celebrate the winner of the Tour de France (still the major cycling event outwith the Olympics).

However, the mystery deepens as Rangers were also gifted a French miners lamp by St Etienne before their 1975 second round European Champions Cup tie (Rangers lost both legs, 2-0 in France and 2-1 at Ibrox) as Saint Étienne went all the way to the final at Hampden only to be beaten by German titans Bayern Munich 1-0.

The bike itself appears to have been made by Manufacture Francaise d'Armes et Cycles de Saint Étienne (translated as French Arms and Cycle Factory of Saint Étienne). The 1957 winner of the Tour de France, Frenchman Jacques Anquetil may have won riding a Manufrance bike whilst the 1975 winner,

Bernard Thévenet, also of France, rode a Peugeout-made cycle.

Whatever the true details it is clear this is a fascinating and intriguing addition to the usual cups and pennants one finds in football club trophy rooms.

35

Death in the Sun

Rangers are a club built on success, delivering silverware and being able to continually dominate their rivals. Chief among those are historical enemies Celtic Football Club, from the East End of Glasgow.

How hard it is then for supporters to have to acknowledge that the club's record defeat came against the team known as 'The Hoops' and for it to happen in a cup final too!

19 October 1957 saw the League Cup Final played at Hampden on a beautifully sunny Glasgow afternoon (kick-off was at 2.45pm). It pitted a Rangers side, managed by Scot Symon and filled with the likes of Caldow, Shearer and Hubbard, against Jimmy McGrory's Celtic side with the likes of Fallon, Fernie and Collins.

Rangers came into the final as league champions whilst Celtic were the League Cup holders. In front of over 82,000 fans, it would be a day the light blue legions would be keen to forget.

Celtic dominated proceedings and raced into a three-goal lead in front of disbelieving eyes. Hopes of a comeback after Rangers scored through Simpson (58) were shattered as Celtic went on to score a further four goals (including a 90th-minute penalty and a hat-trick for Billy McPhail).

Rangers fans demanded action; there were calls for the board, manager and players to depart as expected. Celtic fans enjoyed the bragging rights and soon begun to refer to 'Hampden in the sun, Celtic 7, Rangers 1, but it would be something of a false dawn for them.

Rangers, ever able to face down adversity, would see off any challengers and go on to retain the league championship the following season a full 14 points ahead of their rivals who could only place sixth behind Hearts, Motherwell, Dundee and Airdrie. Celtic would also lose out on the League Cup trophy, being knocked out in the semi-finals by eventual runners-up Partick Thistle.

36

This is Sparta

There was a time when the idea of 'aggregate' and 'away goals' was unknown in European football, when teams played always to win, and a straight shoot-out helped promote attacking football.

1960 saw such an occasion, when Rangers were gifted the 'Sparta vase' by Dutch club Sparta Rotterdam who Rangers faced in the quarter-final of the European Cup.

After a stunning 3-2 away win thanks to goals from Wilson (4), Baird (35) and Murray (63) Rangers welcomed Sparta to Ibrox but were beaten 1-0 in front of an incredible crown of 82,587.

So, to the neutral, winner-takes-all play-off. Arsenal's Highbury was the venue for the game which saw Rangers run out 3-2 victors thanks to two own-goals from unlucky Sparta players (Verhoeven, 26 and Van Der Lee, 70) as well as a strike from Baird (56).

Rangers (First Leg): Niven, Caldow, Davis, Paterson, Little, Stevenson, Scott, McMillan, Murray, Baird, Wilson

Rangers (Second Leg): Ritchie, Caldow, Davis, Little, Stevenson, Paterson, Scott, McMillan, Murray, Baird, Wilson

Rangers (Play-off): Niven, Caldow, Little, Davis, Paterson, Stevenson, Scott, Baird, Millar, Wilson, Brand

37

Spode China Bowl

In the 1961 season England's Wolverhampton Wanderers were one of the European Cup Winners' Cup favourites having won the old English First Division in two of the previous three seasons.

For the first leg of the semi-final at Ibrox they gifted the club this beautiful painted China bowl standing roughly seven inches high.

Rangers had seen off Ferencváros and Borussia Mönchengladbach in the earlier rounds and in front of a huge 80,000 roaring crowd produced a fantastic display to win the first leg 2-0; despite playing with ten men after Harold Davis was unable to overcome an injury early in the first half (this was a time before substitutions were allowed).

The return leg saw Rangers take an enormous travelling support, estimated to be over 10,000. Those who made the trip saw Rangers come away with a 1-1 draw, winning the tie 3-1 on aggregate and making Rangers the first British club to reach a European final although the campaign would end in disappointment against Italy's Fiorentina (although we'd see them again in time).

Rangers (First Leg): Ritchie, Caldow, Davis, Shearer, Paterson, Baxter, Wilson, Scott, Bailie, Brand, Hume

Rangers (Second Leg): Ritchie, Caldow, David, Shearer, Paterson, Baxter, Wilson, Scott, Brand, McMillan, Hume

38

John Greig MBE

In the storied history of Rangers, many men have left their mark upon the club. But only one has consistently been viewed as 'the greatest', even being voted so by the fans in 1999. A player and manager who embodied all the club and support stand for both on and off the pitch, the legendary John Greig.

A 'one club' man, Greig was brought to the club in 1961 after being convinced by his father. He would become *the Ranger*, the pure expression of the talent, desire, success, certainty and strength which defines the club.

As a player he made 857 first-team appearances, winning five league titles, six Scottish Cups and four League Cups, captaining the side on that immortal night in 1972 when the club won its only European trophy to date. He was also awarded an MBE in 1977 for his services to the game. Few records can stand in comparison.

His debut was against Airdrie in the League Cup in September 1961, scoring as Rangers won 4-1.

His first of five championships came in 1962/63 (the others were in 1963/64, 1974/75, 1975/76 and 1977/78) along with his first Scottish Cup as Rangers beat Celtic in a final for the first time in 35 years with a 3-0 victory in a replay.

He received several offers to move to England, but Greig showed that devotion and loyalty so missing in the modern era.

Despite winning their third Scottish Cup in 1966 with a 1-0 defeat of Celtic, it was the next season when Rangers really began to turn the corner. Greig was club captain by now as they enjoyed a European run in the Cup Winners' Cup.

In the black days following the Ibrox disaster when 66 people died in 1971, he became the focal point of a support in mourning, helping to ensure the players attended the victims' funerals and putting his efforts into ensuring the club emanated togetherness in the face of such a shared tragedy that transcended football. His statue resides outside the stadium as a fitting tribute to those fans who lost their lives in the 1971, 1961 and 1902 tragedies.

Greig was 35 and coming toward the end of his career when manager Jock Wallace quit abruptly for Leicester. Fittingly, his last act as a player was to have lifted the Scottish Cup when Aberdeen were beaten 2-1 in the 1977/78 final, before accepting the offer to fill the manager's position.

In his time behind the 'big desk' he delivered two Scottish Cups and two League Cups before he resigned in October 1983 to be replaced by the returning Jock Wallace.

With blue in his veins, however, it was only a matter of time before he and the club returned to each other's embrace. He returned to Ibrox in 1990 as a PR Executive, working alongside Dick Advocaat and in the club's youth department trying to unearth the next young superstar.

He was made a director of the club in December 2003 but stepped down in 2011 during the Craig Whyte era in an attempt to highlight the lack of credibility and transparency in the boardroom. He returned to the club when Dave King and his investors rescued it in 2015.

The term 'legend' is degraded and misused these days, but

John Greig was the real deal. Skilful in his own right, determined in his sense of purpose, unshakeable in his loyalty to the red, white and blue. A winner imbued with the very traits built into the foundation of Rangers Football Club.

The statue of John Greig at Ibrox. *Alamy*

39

Sandy Jardine

Some players embody something more than just football. Maybe it is class, maybe it is resolve in defence of their club, maybe they become a rallying point of calm in a storm.

Sandy Jardine was all of these things, a classy, marauding full-back capable of fantastic goals, an impeccable ambassador for, and defender of, the club as well as being a complete gentleman. He began his career with Rangers in 1965, going on to make over 600 appearances. As well as playing in the club's Cup Winners' Cup triumph in 1972, he added three top-flight titles, five Scottish Cups and five Scottish League Cups.

But those stats tell nothing of the man Sandy Jardine was. Able to win Scotland's player of the year at 37, he also, alongside ex-Ranger Alex MacDonald, almost led Hearts to the league title, missing out through a now infamous defeat to Dundee.

But it was through his off-field activities that he made arguably his greatest contribution. Returning to the club after his managerial foray he served in various capacities, importantly overseeing the archive and trophy room of the club. He, alongside McCoist, was also instrumental in facing down internal and external calls to inexplicably hand back titles won during the years Rangers indulged in the legal use of Employment Benefit Trusts (EBTs). Without the strength of Jardine, hard, legitimately won trophies may have been taken by

Sandy Jardine in action against Celtic in 1978. *Colorsport*

those who couldn't win them on the field of play.

He sadly passed in 2014 after a battle with cancer. Rangers were granted special permission for their players to all wear the number two (his playing number) on their shorts in their first fixture after his death, whilst the tributes that poured in from the football world gave a glimpse of the standing he held.

Then Celtic Chief Executive Peter Lawwell bridged the Old Firm gap in speaking to the press of Jardine, stating, 'He was a very fine man, and it was a privilege to know him. Sandy was widely respected across the game, and he will be sadly missed by us all.' Former teammate Alex Ferguson also spoke of the deep respect he was held in.

But final word goes to McCoist, who, speaking at the time on the Rangers official website, said: 'His achievements both on and off the pitch are second to none and I was honoured to regard him as a friend.

'He gave everything for this great club and worked tirelessly in a number of roles because he wanted to ensure the traditions, history and standards at Rangers were maintained.

'He recently told me he was proud to be a Ranger and wanted to be remembered forever as a Ranger. Well Sandy, you will go down in history as one of the greatest of all time and we will miss you terribly.'

40

King Kai

If you were to ask any Rangers fan what their dream debut goal would be it would be no shock to hear a 'Cup final winner against Celtic'.

Step forward Danish sensation Kai Johansen in the 1966 Scottish Cup Final replay after both sides had played out an initial 0-0 draw in their first attempt to land a killer blow.

Celtic had bagged the first of what would become nine titles in a row and Rangers faced the players who would go on to win the European Cup a year later, making this victory all the more pleasing in retrospect.

The game itself was scrappy, characterised by rough tactics and physicality, with no hiding place for either side on the Hampden turf in front of a near 97,000 crowd. When it came, however, the goal, in the 70th minute, was a thing of beauty. A Willie Henderson shot was cleared by Bobby Murdoch only for it to land invitingly in the path of Johansen who powerfully let fly from 25 yards into the net, sending the blue legions into rapture and landing Rangers their 19th Scottish Cup victory.

Johansen had moved from his native Denmark and was playing for Morton before manager Scot Symon parted with £20,000 to bring him to Ibrox, where the Dane initially struggled to adapt to the style of play and demands. He would go on to settle in nicely, however, and make 238 appearances for Rangers before retiring at the age of 30, always describing that stunning winner as his 'greatest moment in football'.

The game day itself ended in less celebratory fashion when Celtic fans threw bottles and charged celebrating Rangers fans near the St Enoch Hotel resulting in hospitalisations and arrests.

Kai Johansen battles for the ball against Dundee United in 1969. *Colorsport*

41

The Blue Gates

Ask any Rangers fan and they will likely tell you when they pass on it isn't the pearly gates and St Peter they would want to see but the famous blue gates of Ibrox!

The iconic gates currently sit to the side of the Bill Struth main stand and are a constant draw for seasoned fans and newcomers alike to have photographs taken (or to climb to get a peek at the latest new signing!).

The gates have been in several locations over the years as the stadium was renovated, expanded and reworked but are no longer used to allow fans matchday access.

The ornate gates tower over the looker, much like the club does to its rivals. Atop them, wrought in metal, are the words Rangers Football Club Ltd. The keen eye will also spot some bluebells on the main central gate.

Behind these gates lies a club of unparalleled standing, of history, legacy and stature. To be invited through them is to join a family which spans the globe.

42

The Bayern Horse

A beautiful wild white horse resides within Ibrox. Given to the Glasgow giants by German heavyweights Bayern Munich.

The gift, however, is tinged with sadness, from a Rangers perspective at least, presented on 31 May 1967 when Rangers faced the Germans in the European Cup Winners' Cup Final in Nuremburg.

Rangers, managed by Scot Symon and captained by John Greig, performed well against a team full of German internationals but were ultimately undone in extra time by a goal from Franz Roth.

Rangers would get revenge in 1972, however, defeating the Germans 3-1 on aggregate in the semi-finals on their way to winning the trophy and perhaps metaphorically putting a harness on that Bavarian stallion.

Rangers (First Leg): Martin, Johansen, Jardine, Provan, McKinnon, Greig, Henderson, A. Smith, D. Smith, Hynd, Johnston

43

Never Quite Fergie Time

Alex Ferguson. A name now synonymous with the English Premier League and specifically Manchester United. Undoubtedly one of the greatest managers Britain and indeed the game has ever seen.

But before he cemented his place in the history of the Red Devils this Govan-born boy was a childhood Rangers fan who lived the dream of signing for his boyhood club.

Playing as a striker, Ferguson was brought to Ibrox by then manager Scot Symon from Dunfermline for a then Scottish record fee of £65,000 (having previously scored a hat-trick against the Gers).

Ferguson started well enough in a less-than-stellar side. He spent two years at the club, scoring 44 goals in 57 games. However, he left Rangers rather abruptly soon after the 1969 Scottish Cup Final loss against Celtic. Rangers were beaten 4-0 on the day and Ferguson was singled out and blamed for the opening goal when Celtic captain Billy McNeill evaded him at a corner to head home.

In recent years Ferguson has also made allegations he was targeted by people inside the club due to his wife being a practicing Catholic. It is true historically Rangers had a problem with sectarianism, although the club have made great strides in this area, culminating in the recent award-winning inclusivity campaign 'Everyone Anyone'.

He would go on to briefly make provincial club Aberdeen a force both in Scotland and Europe before heading south to Manchester. In his incredible 27-year career at United he amassed no less than 13 Premier League championships. Importantly, he also added two Champions League titles to the Old Trafford trophy room.

Approached several times, a better historical relationship may have seen him return to Ibrox as manager. However, Rangers fans are left to wonder what could have been if 'Fergie' had pulled on the blue blazer and brown brogues of the club uniform.

Alex Ferguson playing for Rangers against Celtic in the
1969 Scottish Cup semi-final at Hampden Park. *Colorsport*

44

Gullane Sands

Who doesn't like a day at the beach? Rangers players, that's who.

Specifically, those who had to suffer through pre-season training sessions on Gullane Sands under legendary manager Jock Wallace in the 1970s.

The sands, found on the southern shore of the Firth of Forth on the east coast of Scotland are notorious for their steep-sided dunes. Wallace, a fitness guru, had discovered the dunes whilst on a picnic with his wife, and regularly had his players train on these, sprinting up and down the dunes to improve strength, speed and stamina.

Nicknamed 'murder hill' these energy-sapping sessions would prepare the team for the rigours of the season ahead with players describing them as 'horrendous' and 'absolutely brutal' but also the reason the team were able to perform to the last minute of games. Many of Wallace's players have referenced these sessions as the reason they were able to continue playing at a high level until their late 30s and early 40s.

Perhaps not a trip to take the beach ball or bucket and spade on though.

45

The News is Blue!

Fans are voracious in their appetite for knowing what is going on about their clubs and the players within them. Rumours, interviews, transfers, all are the stuff of discussions across all platforms in this media-encompassing age.

In 1971 things were a bit more slow-paced but on Wednesday, 4 August that year fans were treated to the first-ever edition of the official newspaper of Rangers FC, the *Rangers News*. It hit newsstands and at 5p became essential reading.

Below is a quiz from that very first edition; you'll find the answers too. Good luck!

1. From which junior team did Rangers sign Alfie Conn?
2. Who did the Gers beat in the final of the 1963/64 Scottish League Cup?
3. Which Rangers player cost £50,000 when bought from St Johnstone?
4. Who were Rangers' first-ever opponents in the European Cup Winners' Cup?
5. In which season did Rangers first win the Scottish Cup?
6. Rangers won every match in what season?
7. Which Rangers player was known as the 'Wee Prime Minister'?
8. Which current Ibrox player was signed from Motherwell?

9. What remarkable feat did Rangers achieve in season 1929/30?

10. Which Ibrox player at one time played for German side Duisburg?

11. Who scored Rangers' winning goal in the 1965/66 Scottish Cup Final replay against Celtic?

12. Which Ranger has a twin brother who plays with Partick Thistle?

13. How many ex-Rangers players (apart from manager Waddell) are now managing Scottish clubs?

14. Who were the three Scandinavians Rangers signed from Morton?

15. When did wee Willie Henderson sign for Rangers?

1.Musselburgh. 2. Morton. 3. Alex MacDonald. 4. Ferencvaros (Hungary, whom they played in the opening round of the 1960/61 competition. 5. 1893/94. 6. 1898/99. 7. Ian McMillan. 8. Peter McCloy. 9. They won everything they could win. 10. Gerry Neef. 11. Kai Johansen. 12. Ronnie McKinnon. 13. Five – Ian McMillan (Airdrie), John Prentice (Dundee), Jerry Kerr (Dundee United), Harry Melrose (Berwick) and Bobby Shearer (Hamilton Accies). 14. Erik Sorensen, Jorn Sorensen and Kai Johansen. 15. 1959.

46

2 January 1971

On 2 January 1971 fans poured into Ibrox for the traditional New Year's Old Firm game. At the end of the match tragedy would strike when fans were crushed as they exited the stadium via the infamous stairway 13.

sixty-six people would lose their lives.

This author and these pages cannot do those who died, nor their family's sense of loss, justice. Some solace may, however, be found in the fact the resulting inquiries mandated safety and operational changes for every stadium in Britain and were adopted abroad too. Through their tragic sacrifice each of the 66 has helped ensure other fans have attended matches and returned home to their loved ones.

Bryan Todd, Robert McAdam, Peter Wright, John Gardiner, Richard Bark, William Thomson Summerhill, George Adams, John Neill, James Trainer.

Richard Douglas Morrison, James Whyte Rae, David Douglas McGee, Robert Colquhoun Mulholland, David Ronald Paton, George McFarlane Irwin, Ian Frew, John Crawford, Brian Hutchison.

Duncan McIsaac McBrearty, Charles John Griffiths Livingstone, Adam Henderson, Richard McLeay, David Cummings Duff, David

Fraser McPherson, Robert Lockerbie Rae, Robert Campbell Grant, John McNeil McLeay.

David Anderson, John Buchanan, John McInnes Semple, John Jeffrey, Robert Maxwell, Matthew Reid, Alexander McIntyre, Peter Gilchrist Farries, Thomas Melville.

John James McGovern, George Wilson, Robert Charles Cairns, Hugh McGregor Addie, James Yuille Mair, Margaret Oliver Ferguson, Robert Turner Carrigan, George Alexander Smith, Walter Robert Raeburn.

Andrew Jackson Lindsay, Charles Dougan, William Mason Philip, Russell Morgan, Peter Gordon Easton, George Crockett Findlay, Charles Stirling, Thomas Dickson, James Graham Gray.

Thomas McRobbie, Ian Scott Hunter, Nigel Patrick Pickup, Russell Malcolm, Alexander Paterson Orr, Thomas Walker Stirling, James William Sibbald, Frankie Dover, Walter Shields, Thomas Grant, William Duncan Shaw, Donald Robert Sutherland.

Their names are recorded at the stadium and are remembered each year by the club and fans on the anniversary of the disaster. Gone but not forgotten, they remain a part of the Rangers family and a tribute to the importance of supporter safety.

47

'Battlefever' – Jock Wallace

What is better than being Rangers manager? Being Rangers manager twice.

The first man to be handed the keys to the manager's office at Ibrox on two separate occasions was Jock Wallace. A physically imposing man, his relationship with the club had started in less celebratory circumstances as he played in goal and was manager for Berwick Rangers in 1967 as they produced one of Rangers' most embarrassing defeats, seeing off a team including the likes of Willie Johnston, John Greig and Willie Henderson 1-0 in the Scottish Cup.

A founding member of Tranent Rangers Supporters' Club in 1952 he was a Rangers fan to his core. Although a caring and charismatic man he is somewhat unfairly encapsulated by the image of a hard taskmaster, the stern visage with clenched fists, but this was a man who was great friends with Johan Cruyff and who moved Alex Ferguson to write in 1994, 'They don't come with giant character and personality like 'Big Man' Jock Wallace anymore.'

He also is synonymous with adding a new phrase to the language of the Rangers fans. Prior to the 1984 Old Firm League Cup Final, on being asked his prediction he replied, 'I fancy us really strongly, we've got the battle fever on.' It was a phrase taken to heart by Rangers fans and teams ever since and

showed Wallace's understanding of promoting a mentality of success and team togetherness.

He joined the club in 1970 as a coach, going on to take the manager role in 1972 after Rangers had clinched the European Cup Winners' Cup. He duly delivered two league championships, Scottish Cup and League Cup trebles in the space of three seasons, in the process ending Celtic's attempt at a record ten leagues in a row. He then left for Leicester, winning them promotion to the old Football League First Division, and via Motherwell before returning to an under-performing Rangers in 1983.

Despite bringing the League Cup back to Ibrox twice these were momentarily flashes of previous greatness and he could not return past glories. Finally, an end was drawn to his second tenure in charge in April 1986 and the curtain descended on Rangers' first ever two-time manager. It is hard not to imagine what could-have-been if not for that abrupt departure for Leicester after such dominant success and whether, like so many, he was ahead of his time in thinking of 'project cycles' well before the 'modern' manager.

A former commando who saw service in Malay and Northern Ireland, Wallace was visionary in terms of his fitness methods in preparing his men for individual battles and indeed the war for trophies, in the process becoming a Rangers icon and hero remembered fondly. He sadly passed in 1996.

Opposite: Jock Wallace before the 1978 Scottish Cup Final against Aberdeen, which Rangers won 2-1. *Colorsport*

48

The European Cup Winners' Cup

In the Ibrox trophy room you'll find a replica of the European Cup Winners' Cup, a rather unimposing trophy which belies its importance and significance in the club's history.

With such a dominance at home, Europe has always been a key arena for Rangers teams to test themselves in, and throughout the club's history they have reached four European finals: the 2008 UEFA Cup Final as well as the Cup Winners' Cup Finals of 1961, 1967 and 1972. That list contains three disappointments, but 1972 isn't one of them as Rangers claimed their only European trophy to date that balmy evening in Barcelona.

24 May 1972 is a date burned into the collective conscience of the Rangers support, arguably the pinnacle of the club's footballing achievements.

Rangers had seen off French side Rennes 2-1 on aggregate in the first round, drawing 1-1 in France before progressing thanks to a 1-0 Ibrox win.

In the second round, Rangers won the first leg at Ibrox 3-2 thanks to goals from Stein (2) and Henderson, before travelling to Portugal. A thrilling game in the original Estádio de Alvalade saw Sporting emerge 4-3 winners on the night, a 6-6 draw overall. Enter Dutch referee, Laurens van Raavens, who ordered a penalty shoot-out which Rangers duly lost out in.

As the Portuguese and their fans celebrated, Rangers players trudged back, heads down, to the away dressing room. As they sat pondering where things had gone wrong, a Scottish journalist popped his head in and politely asked for a chat with manager Wille Waddell. That journalist highlighted the fact that the newly implemented 'away goals' rule should have precluded the need for a penalty shoot-out, as Rangers had edged it in that regard. A conversation with the UEFA officials ensued, the result was overturned, and Rangers were through to the quarter-finals.

Italians Torino lay in wait and were duly dispatched 2-1 on aggregate, Rangers winning at Ibrox after a 1-1 draw in Italy. Things were now getting serious, with German goliaths Bayern Munich the semi-final opponents. However, it also presented a chance for revenge, Bayern having beaten the Gers in the 1967 European Cup Winners' Cup Final.

A Bayern side that contained the likes of Beckenbauer, Hoeness and Roth were held to a 1-1 draw in Germany, Rangers withstanding a heavy barrage from the uber-talented Bavarians. At Ibrox, however, the home support was treated to one of the great European nights, Sandy Jardine and Derek Parlane scoring in the first half which eventually saw Rangers 2-0 victors on the night, winning 3-1 overall. Revenge was sweet!

It was the height of the Cold War, and the final would be an East vs West struggle. From across the Ural Mountains came the might of Dynamo Moscow, in the process becoming the first Russian side to make a European final. The battlefield: the Camp Nou in Barcelona.

The game was breakneck end-to-end stuff before Rangers landed the first blow through a fantastic shot from Colin Stein; the lead was doubled just before half-time when Willie Johnston

The players celebrate in the changing room after their 3-2 victory over Dynamo Kiev in the 1972 Cup Winners' Cup Final. *Colorsport*

headed home. Just four minutes into the second half and all thoughts turned to celebration when Johnston found the net for a second time.

But Russians are not known for giving up. Showing true spirit they roared back into life, scoring two goals, the second just three minutes from time. Hearts beat faster and all eyes turned to the clock.

There, across the noise of the fans came the longed-for high pitch of the final whistle; Rangers had done it! On to the pitch poured the fans in delight. However, this was General Franco's Spain and the militia reacted with extreme violence, triggering scenes which would see the trophy handed to captain John Greig inside the stadium and Rangers banned from Europe for two years (reduced to one after an appeal).

Nothing could stop the celebrations back in Scotland though, and Rangers returned to a heroes' welcome. Finally, the club had conquered in Europe. Ironically, when they next made a European final, it would once again be against Russian opponents.

49

The Moody Blue

Rangers have been graced by incredible talents over the years; names like Baxter, Henderson and Laudrup roll off the tongue. And rightly, in any conversation over the greatest talent, comes the name of the man Dutch superstar Ruud Gullit once described as 'an unbelievable player' and 'one of the greatest players in world football' after coming up against him in a friendly whilst playing for Feyenoord against the Gers. His love of Rangers and home is the only reason more fans didn't have the joy of seeing that wonderful left foot dazzle defenders.

Davie Cooper, once nicknamed the 'moody blue' in a reference to the band and his seeming reluctance to engage with the media, was well known for being untroubled by the thought of 'brand' or media perception but those who knew him best testify to his generosity, love of the game and keenness to help players develop.

I admit to being particularly invested here; Cooper was a player who lit up the game for me on first seeing him. We call it the beautiful game even when so much of it is ugly. Even now, years after his tragic passing at the age of 39, his talent reminds us that beneath the gaudy veneer of over-priced, over-hyped players, the ability to turn your man outside and in remains a gift like no other.

Jock Wallace was mesmerised watching 'Coop' take apart his Rangers side whilst playing against Clyde in the League Cup and convinced the board to pay out a steal of £100,000 in amongst interest from England.

Graeme Souness, after spending time in the manager's chair at Ibrox, confessed, 'If I wasn't so selfish, I would be telling the big clubs in Italy about him, but why would I hunt a talent like that out the door?' Walter Smith famously added, 'God gave Davie Cooper a talent. He would not be disappointed with how it was used.'

An embodiment of the raw spirit of the game, after a successful time with Rangers (winning three league titles, three Scottish Cups and seven League Cups) he went on to help Motherwell lift the Scottish Cup. In later years he successfully coached young players, passing on his wisdom to the up-and-coming generations.

But he will always be a Ranger, scoring famous goals, making mazy runs and leaving defenders wishing they had stabilizers.

In typical laconic fashion, when asked about his time in the light-blue jersey, he cut right to the chase: 'I played for the team I loved.'

50

Crossing the Divide

With a rivalry as intense and historical as the Old Firm, it is no surprise that playing for both clubs is not a common occurrence. Ask any Rangers fan, though, and three cases will probably come to mind.

Alfie Conn was a hero to the blue legions, having helped Rangers to win the European Cup Winners' Cup in 1972, but after leaving Ibrox for Tottenham Hotspur in 1974 he would return to Scotland in 1977, this time to sign for Celtic with whom he would win the double.

Mo Johnston was also a striker but his journey the reverse of Conn's. Adored by the Hoops fans, he was pinched from a return to Parkhead from Nantes by Graeme Souness in 1989, not only surprising Celtic but humiliating them in the process.

Kenny Miller holds the distinction of being the only player to have crossed the divide twice. He originally moved from Hibs to Rangers in 2000, returning between 2008 and 2011 having sandwiched a stint with Celtic during 2006/07 in between.

Playing for both clubs immediately opens the player and their loyalty in the eyes of the fans up to criticism. Can you be a true Ranger if you have pulled on the Hoops? A question to fuel many an evening, although it is telling that no manager has yet taken up the gauntlet.

51

Ready to Lead

In total, 23 men have had the honour of sitting behind the manager's desk, some for only a game or a few months on an interim basis, with two, Walter Smith and Jock Wallace having the distinction of being two-time permanent managers.

Name	Period Active	Nation
James Gossland *	1985–1899	Scotland
William Wilton**	1899–1920	Scotland
Bill Struth	1920–1954	Scotland
Scot Symon	1954–1967	Scotland
David White	1967–1969	Scotland
Willie Waddell	1969–1972	Scotland
Jock Wallace	1972–1978	Scotland
	1983–1986	
John Greig	1978–1983	Scotland
Tommy McLean	1983–1983	Scotland
Graeme Souness	1986–1991	Scotland
Walter Smith	1991–1998	Scotland
	2007–2011	
Dick Advocaat	1998–2001	Netherlands
Alex McLeish	2001–2006	Scotland
Paul Le Guen	2006–2007	France
Ian Durrant	2007–2007	Scotland

Ally McCoist	2011–2014	Scotland
Kenny McDowall	2014–2015	Scotland
Stuart McCall	2015–2015	Scotland
Mark Warburton	2015–2017	England
Graeme Murty	2017–2017	Scotland
	2017–2018	
Pedro Caixinha	2017–2017	Portugal
Jimmy Nicholl	2018–2018	Northern Ireland
Steven Gerrard	2018–	England

*Match secretary
**Previously match secretary but dated here from known official manager status

52

The Drybrough Cup – Cooper's Day

An Old Firm cup final win is always sweet, to score in one ever sweeter. To score a goal for the ages? That is comic-book-level heroics.

The now-defunct Drybrough Cup was a season pre-event for the eight top-scoring teams in the country from the previous campaign.

The game itself was played on a beautiful August day in 1979 and finished 3-1 to Rangers in front of an electrified Hampden crowd of over 40,000. An opener from John MacDonald, a fantastic strike in itself for the debutant but an also-ran compared with what was to come, set the Gers fans into song.

Better was to come when Jardine, defending on his own 18-yard box, had a header dropped to him and stole in ahead of Aitken, controlled the ball and set off across the Hampden turf. Two challenges ridden, he drove on into the Celtic half. Some defenders lock up at that stage, not Jardine. On he went, Rangers fans willing him forward, Celtic fans looking for a challenge. On an on, into the Celtic box, a final dip of the shoulder and he was past McAdam before a swing of his cultured left foot saw the ball nestle in the net. Surely the goal of the game!

Step forward Davie Cooper, who had been targeted for some rough treatment by the Celtic players, and Sandy Jardine's fantastic goal had to settle for second place in the shade.

Some goals echo down the years to the fanbase; some of those for the match they won, some for the 'last-minute-winner' joy, some just for the sheer quality of the strike. These latter goals transcend time, putting smiles on faces for generations yet to come. Each and every young fan has had Cooper's goal passed to them by older bears like a family heirloom. And like many heirlooms, it was utterly priceless.

Alex MacDonald got to the byline and chipped the ball into the Celtic box with Cooper getting in ahead of the Celtic defence, taking it on his chest and flicking it over the head of Roddie McDonald. Two Celtic players then converged on him, another flick into the air and they were left facing a blank space and each other. Breathless fans watched as the ball wasn't even allowed to drop, a cushioned touch taking it away from McAdam before a controlled finish past Latchford in goal.

A special moment from a special player.

53

McCoist – Goals Guaranteed

There once lived a man who had a golden right foot. Then he won his second European Golden Shoe and had the pair.

Take that in, two of them. A Scottish striker, playing in Scotland. That's Ally McCoist MBE, goals guaranteed.

Brought to Rangers by John Greig for £185,000 in 1981 from Sunderland (after rejecting Rangers to sign for the English club) he announced himself by scoring 33 seconds into his Old Firm debut. It was the start of a relationship against Rangers' greatest rivals that would be one-sided and help make Ally a hero to the blue half of Glasgow (he scored 27 goals in that fixture overall).

Super Ally; the goals, the patter, the relentless winning mentality ending with him having more silverware than a 15th century monarch. He stands undoubtedly for many as the greatest penalty box striker Scotland has produced and remains Rangers' record goalscorer (355 goals in 581 appearances). A player adored by the blue legions and secretly yearned for by other teams' fans.

An iconic player, part of the nine-in-a-row mainstays, who scored iconic goals (who else comes off the bench after recovering from a broken leg to score an overhead winner in a cup final?). A record-breaker (who finally lost his Rangers European goals record to Alfredo Morelos in 2021) who played and scored against the best.

After retiring from playing, he returned to the club as assistant manager with Walter Smith in 2007, taking the manager role in 2011 as the club approached financial ruin. Resigned his position when he was unable to bring the club back to the Premiership; however, his passion, commitment and presence held Rangers together during the implosion of 2012. This latter point should never be overlooked or forgotten.

Rangers' golden boy in golden shoes who wrote his own, and the fans', fairy-tale endings time after time, in the process rightly becoming part of the club's history and folklore.

Ally McCoist lifts the league trophy in 1990. *Colorsport*

54

The Liverpool Vase

Standing only 13 and a half inches tall the Liverpool vase marks the beginning of life for something far larger.

Presented to Rangers in December 1981 prior to a friendly with the then reigning European champions, the game marked the completion of the redevelopment of Ibrox with the opening of the Govan Stand.

Rose coloured with the Liverpool crest it was the only gift Rangers received that evening as they went down 2-0 to goals from Dalglish and Whelan in front of over 40,000 fans.

The vase has taken on more meaning recently with the appointment of Liverpool legend Steven Gerrard as Rangers manager and is one of many instances of a relationship between both clubs of respect and support.

Rangers: Stewart, Jardine, McAdam, Dawson, Jackson, Cooper, Bett, Russell, Dalziel, MacDonald, Redford

55

Cult Kitman – Jimmy Bell

Every team needs the support of dedicated and loyal staff, Rangers are no different and have a cult hero amongst fans in kitman Jimmy Bell.

His official start date with the club is debatable, but most agree it was just prior to the Graeme Souness revolution in 1986. A Rangers fan to the core, he was initially the club's coach driver before taking on kit duties.

A legend around the club he has seen thousands of players come and go (as well as his fair share of managers) and remains a firm favourite of the support and the squad.

The keeper of the jerseys, the dressing room mainstay, to those he likes he is simply 'Jimmy'.

56

A Moustachioed Iconoclast

'So, gentlemen, can I just say to you, welcome our new player-manager, Graeme Souness.' A simple sentence delivered by Chief Executive David Holmes, but which started off a complex chain reaction shaking Rangers, and Scottish football, to their cores and catapulting both into the modern era.

It was April 1986, three full years before the fall of the Berlin Wall. But here was revolution on our doorstep as Souness swapped Sampdoria for Ibrox. It was a first-ever managerial job for the Liverpool legend.

The look, the moustache, the tan, the charisma, is it any wonder Rangers fans fell in love immediately?

He joined as player-manager with an emphasis on the latter, making his debut against Hibs at Easter Road, lasting 37 minutes before being caught up in a melee and receiving a red card, helping Hibs to a win. All in he'd make 55 appearances, scoring five goals.

Whilst still a world-class midfielder who treated fans to glimpses of his rare talent, it was his managerial role where he would create a lasting legacy.

He inherited a sleeping giant; success had been thin on the ground during the past decade and the league championship had eluded Ibrox for nine years.

Taking advantage of the banning of English clubs from European football following the Hysel disaster, as well as the fact the club's facilities were beyond most English outfits, Souness, first with Holmes and then with David Murray, was able to bring in top talent from south of the border such as England captain Terry Butcher and goalkeeper Chris Woods, rebuilding from scratch after keeping on five players from an inherited squad of around 30.

But that wasn't the only change in the air. Souness, like Holmes, had no respect for historical Protestant/Catholic divides, winning was their religion and they would have no heretics. Holmes himself had set the scene early on when being asked the religion of Woods at his unveiling. He left nothing to doubt, replying, 'If you have a sectarian policy, you ask it, we haven't asked it. I'm trying to make a point here. We aren't curious.'

Souness would similarly and spectacularly rip up the previous tenets of the Scottish game and leave no one in doubt that Rangers no longer cared about such things when he signed ex-Celtic star and known Catholic Mo Johnston in 1989.

On the footballing front he also delivered, the league title was duly won in his maiden season along with the League Cup (thanks to a 2-1 victory over Celtic). The decade of hurt was over, Rangers could look to the future and although Celtic would wrestle the title back in the following season the tide had turned. It would leave the hoops marooned and desolate.

The title was duly reinstalled at Ibrox in season 1988/89 and the trophy must have felt at home because it refused to leave for another eight years!

Toward the end of the 1989/90 season, as Rangers sought to consolidate with a second successive title win, Souness was feeling the pressure and focus in Scotland personally. There had been touchline bans, scrapes with the SFA and an absurd bust-up with a tea lady. His health was also suffering; within 12 months of leaving Rangers he would undergo open-heart surgery.

There was only one club which could have tempted him, the place where he was, and still is, revered as much as in Govan: Liverpool. They duly came calling before the end of the season and, with his mind made up, he informed David Murray, expecting to be given the chance to see out the league campaign. That hunger to end on a high wouldn't be satisfied, however, with Murray announcing his departure and installing assistant Walter Smith (who would win the title) as permanent manager.

A transformative figure for Rangers and Scottish football, maybe even Scottish society, Graeme Souness remains to the Rangers faithful, that 'magnificent bastard'.

Graeme Souness in action against Tottenham Hotspur in 1986. *Colorsport*

57

Kiev Samovar

Russian clubs have always had an air of mystique around them, possibly a hangover of the Cold War, the barbed wire, Berlin Wall and secret-agent skulduggery.

Graeme Souness was to show his own James Bond-esqe strategic counter-intelligence against the Russian champions Dynamo Kiev during the 1987/88 European Cup first round encounter when the 12-and-a-half-inch high silver samovar (a Russian teapot or urn) was gifted.

Kiev made up the majority of the Russian national team at this time with players such as Anatoliy Demianenko and Oleh Blokhin and were considered strong favourites. Rangers did well to leave Russia with only a 1-0 defeat having played in front of a huge 100,000 partisan crowd.

Enter agent Souness. Having noticed in the first leg how Dynamo liked to get the ball wide and play expansive football he (much to the Russians' dismay) had the Ibrox pitch narrowed by a few yards!

Rangers, now restricting Dynamo's space and ability to flood forward, roared on by their own partisan crowd won on the night 2-0 to win the tie overall 2-1 on aggregate. Many fans still recall the atmosphere as one of the best Ibrox has ever seen.

Interestingly, both Oleh Kuznetsov and Oleksiy

Mykhailychenko from that Dynamo squad would go on to play for Rangers.

Rangers (First Leg): Woods, Nicholl, Roberts, Phillips, Souness, Butcher, Ferguson, Cohen, McGregor, Durrant, McCoist

Rangers (Second Leg): Woods, Nicholl, Phillips, Souness, McGregor, Butcher, Francis, Cohen, Durrant, McCoist

Rangers goalscorers Ally McCoist and Mark Falco celebrate after their side's 2-0 European Cup victory over Dynamo Kiev at Ibrox in 1987.

58

5-1 Fun in the sun

'Heaven for the Gers', 'Rampant Rangers', these were some of the headlines following an incredible Old Firm match at Ibrox in August 1988. The title of this piece has somewhat spoiled the outcome, yes it was sunny. Oh, it also finished with Rangers handing out a 5-1 thrashing to the Hoops.

Rangers went into the match off the back of a less-than-morale-boosting 0-0 draw with Hibs in the type of game one watches glassy-eyed, praying to the gods of football for any type of goal.

Over 44,000 were packed into the stadium and it was the green-and-white hordes who found their voice first when Celtic scored in the first five minutes thanks to Frank McAvennie being in the right place to tap home after Peter Grant had hit the bar. In a testament to his later career, McAvennie knew exactly where to find treasure in the box.

Rangers were wounded, but as the saying famously goes, 'If you want to hit the king you need to kill the king.' Celtic had struck a blow, but it was far from a mortal one.

Within minutes Rangers' own treasure hunter Ally McCoist had struck gold, firing home after John Brown's effort had been blocked. Rangers settled in and began to dominate proceedings with chance after chance spurned through wasteful finishing or the intervention of lady luck.

Then, ten minutes from the break, she decided to reward the Gers fans for their patience by allowing them a glimpse of sublime beauty with a goal dubbed 'made in England'. Gary Stevens poured in a long throw, Terry Butcher up from the back nodded it on and a Celtic player headed it away from goal into the path of the majestic midfield maestro Ray Wilkins. With the touch and technique that had taken him from Chelsea to Manchester United then AC Milan, he struck the sweetest of volleys from around 20 yards. Andrews in the Celtic goal may as well have been 10ft tall for all it would have helped. You can clearly see a jubilant Ally McCoist saying 'what a goal' to Wilkins, and I think we would all agree!

In front but still hungry, Rangers piled on the pressure as Celtic wobbled with cracks showing half-time couldn't come quick enough. The teams went in with Rangers ahead by one.

But those 15 minutes pass quickly when you know the other team have your scent and, before they could properly organise, Celtic were back on the pitch and 3-1 down after McCoist had sent a looping header over the hapless Andrews with Kevin Drinkell in attendance to add pressure.

'More!' came the cries from the Rangers fans, who sensed Rangers could hand out one of those Old Firm lessons both sets of support crave. Walters, McCoist, Drinkell, Wilkins; Celtic couldn't live with them, and cracks were becoming chasms. Little surprise then when an hour in Walters, in a trademark show of skill that twisted his marker out of shape, whipped over a ball for Drinkell to power home a header. Even sweeter was to come from Walters as he used all his skills to silence the racist abuse he confirmed in his autobiography he had received from the away support.

Within minutes it was five; Aitken dithered, McCoist nipped in and broke into the box only for Aitken to compound his mistake by pulling him down. Before the referee could award the required penalty, the ball broke to Walters who neatly tucked it away into the bottom corner.

Rangers were rampant and played out the last half an hour with a composure and dominance which would be the hallmark of the coming decade. There was frustration, however, at full time from the likes of McCoist and Durrant that the team hadn't capitalised and overhauled that 7-1 Old Firm Celtic record.

Ray Wilkins sadly passed in 2018.

Ray Wilkins in 1988. *Colorsport*

59

David Murray

'For every £5 Celtic spend we will spend £10,' so spoke Rangers owner David Murray in bombastic fashion in 2000.

In hindsight, the comment smacks of Greek-tragedy levels of hubris, and certainly Murray is a study in believing one's own hype to the exclusion of reality. In truth, his is a story of glorious success followed by avoidable disaster and reputational ruin. But it also contains a lesson for the fanbase in questioning authority.

Murray bought the club for £6m in November 1988 from then owner Lawrence Marlborough. Fans rejoiced as the entrepreneur seemed like the right man to drive the club forward. In later years, he was keen to be seen as the man who brought Graeme Souness to Scotland (he wasn't, that was Marlborough) and on a more tangible level then vice-chairman David Holmes, who had kept the club running in great shape.

Murray set about backing first Graeme Souness and then Walter Smith with talents such as Woods, Hateley, Butcher, Laudrup and Gascoigne. Wages and transfer fee records were routinely set then broken during a period of free spending. Under Murray's stewardship, Rangers won a total of 15 league titles and 26 cups, but any tangible success in Europe, the ultimate aim, eluded him.

He was unrivalled (and possibly ahead of his time) in terms of commercial activity, signing long-term deals with the likes of

JJB Sports, calling on fans to 'buy direct', commercialising every aspect he could and convincing businessmen such as Dave King and Joe Lewis' ENIC to invest (the latter would ask to put his own man on the Rangers board and in doing so would give a young Daniel Levy, now Tottenham Hotspur Chief Executive, his first role in football).

When Wim Jansen's Celtic stopped Rangers' attempt at securing a tenth title in a row Murray doubled down; Walter Smith exited the manager's office and in came the club's first foreign manager, Dutchman Dick Advocaat. Murray backed his man to claim back dominance and progress in Europe with unprecedented funds (spending £12m on the likes of Tore Andre Flo) simultaneously landing the club with unprecedented levels of debt (at one point passing the £70m mark).

He also instigated the use of EBTs, a completely legitimate tax vehicle but something that would come to haunt Rangers in the coming decades.

Despite reclaiming the title and playing arguably the finest football ever to be seen at Ibrox, Advocaat was unable to make serious inroads in Europe and left the club just as the financial constraints started to bite.

Alex McLeish stabilised the team and retuned them to winning ways before a failed experiment with French manager Paul Le Guen. Murray had one last masterstroke, however, convincing Walter Smith to leave the Scotland manager role to rescue his boyhood club.

Smith immediately delivered trophies and in 2008 gave Murray the European run he had long chased, going all the way to the UEFA Cup Final before eventual defeat (ironically Dick Advocaat managed the opposing Zenit St Petersburg).

However, a final nail was driven into the coffin of Rangers' financial position with the 2008 global credit crunch which saw Murray's non-football businesses suffer £100m-plus losses. Lloyds Banking Group effectively took over running of the club.

He finally sold the club to Crag Whyte for £1, leading directly to the eventual liquidation of the club's holding company. Something most fans will never forgive.

A hubristic egoist, he delivered success on an unparalleled level and created the financial conditions which allowed Rangers to attract the best talent. Something that led to few fans questioning the means and methods he employed. The memories those players provided will live on. However, an owner's first duty when it comes to an institution of Rangers' size is to protect its ongoing future. In that he failed spectacularly and as such is rightly held in contempt by the support.

60

The Katowice Black Vase

One of the most striking gifts Rangers have ever received was from Polish club GKS Katowice in 1988.

Rangers met the Poles in the UEFA Cup first round, running out 1-0 winners at Ibrox thanks to a Mark Walters goal before seeing off a spirited Katowice side 4-2 away.

Standing 17 inches high the vase is more art than trophy. It is carved from a single piece of coal in a homage to the mining heritage of the Katowice area.

Perhaps it is the shared working-class background Glasgow shares with the Polish region, or a hark back to a time of heavy industry when Rangers were formed that makes this particular gift catch the eye.

Rangers (First Leg): Woods, Stevens, Brown, Gough, Wilkins, Butcher, Drinkell, Ferguson, Cooper, Durrant, Walters

Rangers (Second Leg): Woods, Munro, Gough, Stevens, Wilkins, Butcher, Cooper, Ferguson, Walters, Durrant, McCoist

61

MoJo

It is common knowledge that, historically, Rangers as a club did not wish to sign players who practised the Roman Catholic faith. This was a stance born of the entrenched societal views of its time and the legacy and history of the club, incorporating the 'Irish question' and ideas of nationhood, including mass migration to Scotland from both Eire and Northern Ireland.

Whilst such prejudices are now firmly in the past for the club, there was a crystalline moment when they emerged from this self-imposed embargo on Catholic players and decided to join the modern world. Even now the name echoes down through Scottish football history and has become shorthand for radical progressive change for some, and a lesson in how to humiliate your rivals for all time for others.

On 10 July 1989 Rangers unveiled a new signing: Maurice Johnston, nicknamed 'MoJo' was a prolific Scottish striker who was plying his trade for French side Nantes. Nothing controversial in that, you may think, but the move shook Scottish football to its core and left Rangers' arch rivals with red-white-and-blue egg on their face.

Graeme Souness had swept into the manager's job at Ibrox determined to eschew old views in the ruthless pursuit of silverware. Problematic views on religion would not stop him signing the best players for Rangers, outdated quasi-religious exclusion had been replaced by a straight meritocracy. Johnston was a Catholic and had once blessed himself in front of the Rangers support when sent off in a League Cup Final. It mattered not a jot. Rangers had taken a great leap forward.

What made the signing all the sweeter was that Celtic had been chasing Johnston and believed they had their man. Publicity photos had been staged with him holding their jersey and then manager Billy McNeill and the Celtic fans had begun to think on what his goals could mean in the title race to come. Little did they realise those goals would come in a blue jersey as no contract had been signed and Rangers did what big clubs always do, push out rivals and get the job done.

Not all Rangers fans were pleased: however. There were protests, pledges to return season tickets and the obligatory thrown scarf but the tide had turned, and MoJo did his best to ingratiate himself with the blue legions when he scored a winner against Celtic at Ibrox. Goals can negate anything, and Johnston racked up a total of 46 in 100 appearances.

He was not the first known Catholic to have played for the club, but certainly the most high-profile. Often not given the credit for how personally difficult the decision must have been, Johnston, along with Souness and Rangers, in one single stroke publicly moved Scotland past the idea of religion as a transfer factor. That is a legacy to be proud of.

62

Ol' Blue Eyes

A simple note of thanks, it is something neglected in these modern times. But one, from arguably the greatest singer of all time, would wind its way to then Rangers manager Graeme Souness in 1990.

Frank Sinatra, Ol' Blue Eyes, famed for hits such as 'My Way' and 'New York, New York', was 74 when he took to the Ibrox pitch but was still able to hold the crowd in the palm of his hand.

1990 saw Glasgow named the European city of culture, and people were being given the chance to listen to the master crooner who hadn't performed in Scotland for nearly 40 years after some ill-thought concerts which had been panned.

The concert itself suffered from pricing and logistical problems, with some fans paying £60 each for the best seats in front of the stage. Even the cheapest seats were set at £35 with the promoters soon realising that the hoped-for sales were never going to materialise. A very late decision was taken to only use the Govan Stand which cut the overall concert capacity to 11,000. This meant that fans who had paid for those £60 seats now found themselves moved to cheaper areas.

Logistical problems then marred the concert as queues began to build up outside leaving thousands locked out of the ground as Sinatra took to the stage, with some fans not getting inside until five or six songs into the set. Refunds were handed out, but it was hardly compensation for missing the show. No one was spared as even Souness himself discovered – his £60 seats were reportedly occupied by someone else, leaving him having to watch from an Ibrox hospitality suite.

But classy to the last, Sinatra wowed the crowd who were there and followed it up with that thank you note.

63

The Goalie

Rangers have had many a fine goalkeeper down the years: McGregor, McCloy, Klos, Woods; all fantastic keepers in their own right and worthy of all the acclaim they receive.

However, the greatest is the man known simply to all as 'the goalie': Andy Goram, who could easily also lay claim to being the finest goalkeeper ever to play in Scotland. Celtic manager Tommy Burns had this to say after yet another stellar Old Firm display, 'If anyone gets round to doing my tombstone, it will have to read: "Andy Goram Broke My Heart."'

Walter Smith's first signing back in 1991, Rangers splashed £1m on the then Hibs goalkeeper. It would prove to be an utter, undisputed bargain. It could have been so different, however. Goram was a talented cricketer and is the only person in history to have both played in a first-class cricket match and gain a full international cap for Scotland at football.

A rocky start with some mishaps was soon overcome, with a string of heart-stopping saves and incredible performances from Goram helping the club to six league titles, three Scottish Cups and three League Cups. Who can ever forget the save from Celtic's Dutch striker Pierre van Hooijdonk in a pulsating and nerve-obliterating 3-3 Old Firm draw in November 1995 in front of a packed Ibrox?

Picture the scene: Goram, tending goal in front of the away fans packed into the Broomloan Road stand, watches as a

challenge from Gough nips the ball. It heads out to Celtic's Tosh McKinlay who sends in a fantastic cross to meet Van Hooijdonk a mere six yards from goal, who hits a clean, crisp volley. A mid-air adjustment, outstretched arm and strong hand, and out went the ball for a corner. The only sound louder than the cheering was thousands of Celtic fans' hearts breaking.

Once transfer-listed by Walter Smith due to fitness and disciplinary issues, the legendary gaffer took Goram to Manchester United (where he played two games for the Red Devils) when Smith agreed to support Alex Ferguson as assistant for a few months. In 2001, Goram would admit to having suffered from gambling and alcohol issues.

The Goalie, the greatest, and that save; remember it the next time someone mentions Gordon Banks; his doesn't even come close in comparison to Andy's.

Opposite: Andy Goram against Celtic in January 1996. *Alamy*

64

Walter OBE

There was a standing joke amongst the support when Rangers began to succumb to financial pressures and the imploding Paul Le Guen experiment ran into difficulty and became listless. It ran along the lines of 'somewhere, a freshly pressed cardigan is being pulled on'. The target of the good-natured jibe over his sartorial choice was Walter Smith. A Rangers managerial great but a man fans and players have always seen as a father figure, a trusted and integral piece of the Rangers landscape. That wouldn't be to mistake his authority which was total.

Smith had taken over the role originally in 1991 when Graeme Souness departed to manage Liverpool, stepping up from Assistant Manager. He clinched the title and over the following seven seasons would etch his name into legend.

A modern incarnation of the spirit, if not methods, of Struth, like Waddell and Wallace his ruthless grip on Scottish football was defining for a generation. People grew up and the world changed during the dominance he brought to Ibrox.

After taking over and winning Rangers' second successive title he then added a further seven more, equalling the Scottish record for consecutive championships. In between he found time to add three Scottish Cups and three League Cups, achieving the domestic treble in the 1992/93 season as well as narrowly missing out to Marseille (later convicted of match-fixing) on reaching the inaugural Champions League Final.

That European season aside, Rangers were not the force abroad they were domestically, occasionally hampered by the now repealed 'three foreigner rule' whereby clubs could only play three foreign players in European games. It was a rule which favoured clubs from bigger nations.

Leaving, sadly, at the end of the 1997/98 season empty-handed, no fan begrudged him a barren year such was the deep affection enjoyed by the man simply known as 'Walter'.

He moved to English club Everton before accepting the offer of the Scottish manager's role in 2004, spending some time as Assistant Manager of Manchester United at Alex Ferguson's request.

In 2008 with the club on the verge of implosion following financial issues and the abrupt exit of Frenchman Paul Le Guen, chairman David Murray called on the Rangers man to help save the club's fortunes.

Very much in the spirit of Willie Waddell's 'Once a Ranger', Walter could not refuse the distress call and took up the challenge. Over the next three years he would move from 'great' to 'legendary' status, re-energise the club and solidify his claim to be the greatest manager Rangers have ever had.

Against a backdrop of never-before-seen cost-cutting at the club, Smith led a functional Rangers team to the UEFA Cup Final. Although defeated, ultimately the prestige had returned to the club and memories were made for a lifetime. It was only the fourth European final in Rangers' history.

He added three more league titles, two Scottish Cups and three League Cups before retiring for good in 2011. Drawn into the internal warfare of the Charles Green and Craig Whyte eras, he was part of a consortium which looked to purchase the club before taking a place on the board.

In such a storied history few have the ability, drive and talent to indelibly etch their name on the club. It was fitting that he signed off with a title win, 5-1 at Kilmarnock on a day affectionately known as 'helicopter Sunday'.

He rightly takes his place amongst the great of Rangers, unparalleled in the modern era he remains the benchmark for success and how a Rangers manager should conduct himself.

© Alamy

65

Champions League Stars

Since the end of the Second World War, when travel across the continent of Europe become possible again, football has been about two things: winning at home and abroad.

Nothing more epitomises the modern game than Europe's premier club competition, the Champions League. To win it is to access its riches but, more importantly, to fans, at least, if not modern chairmen, is the prestige. To see your club up against the best the continent can provide, to travel to far-flung corners and come back victorious. It is the stuff of club mythology and fan legend, to return from Europe with a trophy is to cast oneself in bronze, an immortal of your club's history.

It is also a rite of passage for fans, the trip abroad, by any transport means necessary. Many a story of dodgy bars, ludicrous happenstance and friendships are attached to each European trip.

In the modern era no fan can mistake hearing 'The champions . . . da da daaaaa!' as the logo of eight stars come together to make a football. Composed by Tony Britten, in the style of George Frederic Handel, it was performed by the Royal Philharmonic Orchestra and sung by the Academy of St Martin-in-the-Fields chorus. It uses the three official languages of the Union of European Football Associations (UEFA) – English, German and French.

So, where does Rangers figure in all of this? Well, each of the eight stars in that logo represents a founding member of the Champions League, and Rangers is one of them.

The Champions League was born in 1992, prior to that the top European club competition had been the European Cup. Rangers came together with other top European clubs to found the Champions League, with the aim of helping to establish a better format for clubs and fans. A real driving force behind the initiative was then club secretary Campbell Ogilvie, who helped to overcome initial reticence for change from UEFA president Lennart Johansson and general secretary Gerhard Aigner who rejected the idea twice.

The formation helped stymie the threats of then AC Milan owner Silvio Berlusconi who was threatening to set up his own European Super League (a venture which may ring some recent bells). Alongside Rangers, the other founding members were PSV Eindhoven, Marseille, AC Milan, IFK Gothenburg, Porto, Club Brugge and CSKA Moscow.

The rest as they say, is history.

66

The Battle of Britain – Leeds

In the early 90s, the Champions League was in its infancy. The modern reader may struggle with the fact that only actual 'champions' of a country were included, no averages or co-efficient guaranteeing fifth-placed teams a place at the table.

So, when Rangers and Leeds United met in the second round on 21 October 1992 and 4 November 1992 it was a true meeting of champions, and immediately dubbed the 'Battle of Britain'. This was before TV money revolutionised the English game, so the teams were on a level playing field. Talent, not money, would decide this one.

Leeds were a very good side, boasting talent such as Gary McAllister (now Rangers' assistant manager), French icon Eric Cantona and Lee Chapman.

The first leg at Ibrox started in less than hopeful fashion, McAllister silencing the home crowd early on with a super strike in the first minute. However, an own goal from Leeds' goalkeeper John Lukic (punching into his own net from a corner) put Rangers back in it. A close-range McCoist effort gave Rangers a slender lead to take to Elland Road.

Leeds fans, and the combined English media, gave Rangers no hope of holding on to their lead, expecting the Premier League side to overturn the deficit and progress.

But Rangers had other ideas and produced one of their

most complete and memorable European performances. Mark Hateley mirrored McAllister by hitting an early strike for the Scottish champs when he scored a sensational goal in the opening two minutes, an incredible volley from outside the box, and McCoist bagged a second with a beautiful header after a textbook counter-attack. Andy Goram in the Rangers goal was fantastic and kept Leeds at bay with a string of top saves until Cantona pulled one back late.

But Rangers held their nerve to silence the pundits and the home fans, securing their place in the first-ever Champions League proper and becoming 'Champions of Britain'.

Rangers' Mark Hateley rises above Leeds United's
Chris Whyte during the 1992 match at Elland Road. *Alamy*

67

Broxi Bear

Every club needs a mascot, something (or someone) to cajole the crowd and be a focus, especially for younger fans.

Given Rangers' home is Ibrox, and fans are known affectionally as 'bears' is it any wonder the mascot is called Broxi Bear?

A brown bear, Broxi made his debut in a 2-2 draw against Raith Rovers in November 1993 (Mark Hateley with a double for Rangers on the day).

Broxi has also added to Rangers' history of success, winning the 2002 Disney Channel Mascot Cup.

With his spouse Roxi and their child Boris, you will always find them at Ibrox every other Saturday cheering on the boys in blue!

68

Poor Chick

Walter Smith is known for his even temper and coolness in front of the media, but BBC sports correspondent Chick Young encountered the legendary gaffer's tougher side in a leaked video interview fans got to enjoy!

Smith had brought in the likes of Danish class act Brian Laudrup and European Cup winner Basile Boli in the summer of 1994 with a view to continuing domestic dominance and progressing abroad, after a disappointing Champions League qualifying round defeat to Greek side AEK Athens.

Chick questioned the ability and talent of those signings and, in terms rather blue, Walter (and later assistant Archie Knox) put him straight. Poor Chick couldn't backtrack fast enough but took it in good humour and gave fans a glimpse of what goes on to the edit room floor.

A salutary lesson to journalists everywhere, mind your questions! As at 2021 the BBC currently refuse to send a correspondent to cover Rangers games at Ibrox as part of a dispute over coverage.

69

The Great Dane

Football is the dance to the music of the heart, someone once said. In that case, Brian Laudrup was a tango to techno music at 100bpm. An orchestra of self-expression so missing in today's game that his name reverberates through the fanbase as strongly as it did before he departed for Chelsea in 1998 on a free transfer. Occasionally he is simply 'Godrup', choir optional.

It is impossible to overstate his impact on the Scottish game after Walter Smith lured the Dane from Fiorentina (having been on loan at AC Milan) for £2.3m in the summer of 1994. He had come from footballing stock, his father, Finn and brother Michael, played for Denmark. At one point Brian admitted to considering a life outside of the game due to the pressures of coming from a football family and the comparisons with his brother: 'Having to live up to these expectations was very tough and I have to admit at times I was flirting with the thought of giving up football and doing something else.' He did unofficially quit football at age 15 for ten days. Rangers' fans can only thank the gods of football he didn't stick to it!

Starting in Germany with Bayer Uerdingen at the age of 20, his performances earned him a move to Bavarian titans Bayern Munich after one season, in the process becoming the most expensive player in the Bundesliga. Bayern was not a happy place and he soon moved to Fiorentina; however, that too (including a loan spell at AC Milan) did not give Laudrup the natural footballing home he craved. He did, however, in amongst the unhappiness, play an integral part in Denmark's unbelievable European Championship victory in 1992, when they had been called in at the last minute to replace Yugoslavia (who had qualified) but could not take part due to civil war.

Walter Smith told him he would be integral to Rangers, given a 'free role' and able to express himself. He meant it and Brian finally had a feeling that Ibrox could be the home he had searched the continent for.

His ability to light up games became immediately clear; defenders to this day still in traction from the twisting and turning. Fabulous goals, such as an audacious chip from the byline against Aberdeen and killer finishes against Celtic. Who else could play so brilliantly in a Scottish Cup Final 5-1 rout of Hearts that the final is known as the 'Laudrup game' even though Rangers striker Gordon Durie got a hat-trick?

All were testament to that natural ability, but he had the desire and fight to go alongside, taking the rough treatment in his stride.

But his moment of moments came at Tannadice in May 1997, when he rose to meet a Charlie Miller cross and in powering the ball into the net secured nine-in-a-row, in the process powering his name into immortality.

For four years Rangers and Scotland were blessed with his mercurial talent (he turned down a move to Barcelona early in his Rangers career) before he went to Chelsea in a move he now describes as a mistake. A player to excite, a talent to inspire awe, for those who were there the memories still make the heart skip a beat.

70

Gazza

What makes fans take players to their hearts? Talent, goals, big saves; all of these matter, but are the bread and butter of the professional player. What makes them loved? The sense that they adore the game as the fans do and just occasionally allow the fans to see a glimpse of the sheer child-like joy of playing the game.

Such was Paul Gascoigne. Paul 'Gazza', 'daft as a brush', 'mad as a hatter', 'once in a generation talent' Gascoigne. In amongst the talent and fun were also serious alcohol problems and domestic violence charges, the club resisting the calls to release the player.

The Englishman was brought to Ibrox in a wave of publicity by Walter Smith in July 1995, moving from Italian side Lazio for £4.3 million. Many fans still recall the unveiling, the bleached blonde hair, the smile and the realisation on the face of Gazza as he took in the fans who thronged Edmiston Drive of what he had let himself in for.

On-field genius, goals and controversy followed, such was the ongoing, often self-inflicted drama around Paul Gascoigne who in his own words enjoyed his happiest footballing times at Ibrox. Who else would be booked by a referee after playfully simulating booking him when the ref dropped his yellow card? Scottish refs obviously not known for their sense of humour.

Scoring early against Celtic always helps endear you to the Rangers faithful and Gazza did just that with a deft finish after a lung-bursting run in September that year. Further goals against all-comers followed, including Celtic and a notable performance in a 4-3 cup final win over Hearts, but Gazza kept his best performance for the penultimate day of what would become the eight-in-a-row season in May 1996.

Aberdeen came to Ibrox on that sunny day looking to spoil the party and took the lead through Brian Irvine, much to the shock of the blue masses. Enter the Geordie; within two minutes of that goal a shimmy and mazy solo run from the edge of the box saw him lift the ball over Watt in the Aberdeen goal. 1-1. In the second half Gazza knocked it up a gear and, starting from his own half, ran the length of the field, beating two players and holding off two more before blasting it into the net. 2-1. A penalty sealed the three points (after Gordon Durie was fouled in the box) and in the words of commentator Gerry McNee, 'the hat-trick of the championship'.

Eight-in-a-row was in the bag.

Gazza would leave for Middlesbrough after one more successful season and in later years would publicly state it was his greatest regret. A complete genius on the pitch and completely flawed human being off it.

71

Van Vossen – Oh My Goodness

Players can make, or break, their Rangers careers on games against Celtic. For the unfortunate attacker Peter van Vossen, it was the latter.

The Dutch international was brought to Ibrox by Walter Smith from Turkish club Istanbulspor in January 1996 with rivals Celtic having tried and failed to land him.

Van Vossen was a good player, of that there is no doubt, and he scored his fair share of goals, netting against the likes of Alania Vladikavkaz, Hibs, Clyde and Partick Thistle in the process. But on 11 November 1996 at Parkhead he missed a sitter for the ages.

The game itself had almost everything: a Laudrup goal, a Celtic and Rangers penalty save apiece, even a fox darting out of the stands and on to the pitch at one point (he wasn't wearing club colours so no one could claim him). Rangers secured the three points, but all the talk was of Van Vossen. He chipped the ball forward himself onto a run from Jorg Albertz and kept pace with the German into the Celtic box. With Celtic keeper Stewart Kerr in no-man's land, Albertz squared to Van Vossen, eight yards out with the goal gaping. A slight bobble, a mishit and over the bar it went to everyone's dismay. Commentator Martin Tyler's shocked words summed it up: 'Oh my goodness!'

There have always been misses but that one stands as one of Rangers' worst.

72

The Fans

The Teddy Bears, The Blue Legions, The People. Just some of the names for the incredible Rangers support; rivals have more derogatory terms but these, as expected, are born out of frustration and envy of the unmitigated success of the club and its followers.

'Every other Saturday down the Copland Road' goes the song and it remains the case as Ibrox continues to be filled with demand continually outstripping supply (who else would suffer financial demotion and then set European attendance records?). But the community of Rangers fans is more than just matchday, there is not a point on the globe you will not find a hospitable Rangers Supporters' Club (RSC) with the largest being NARSA (North American Rangers Supporters' Association) and ORSA (Oceania Rangers Supporters' Association). And when it comes to following the team, from Florida to the frozen Russian tundra, it's the fans who have kept 'the blue flag flying high'.

They have also been part of record-making and record-breaking while following the club:

1925: Celtic v Rangers (Scottish Cup semi-final) 101,714
First six-figure crowd for a domestic club game in Scotland.

1928: Celtic v Rangers (Scottish Cup Final) 118,115
Record crowd for a domestic match in Scotland at that time.

1930: Queens Park v Rangers 95,722
World-record crowd for a match involving an amateur team.

1948: Rangers v Hibs (Scottish Cup semi-final) 143,750
Record attendance for a non-final match.

1948: Rangers v Morton (Scottish Cup Final & replay) 129,176 & 133,570
Largest combined attendance for a final plus replay.

1963: Rangers V Morton (League Cup Final) 105,907
First six-figure crowd for a League Cup Final.

1965: Celtic v Rangers (League Cup Final) 107,609
All-time record attendance for a British league cup final.

1973: Rangers v Celtic (Scottish Cup) 122,714
Last 100,000-plus crowd for any football match in the United Kingdom.

2012: Rangers v East Stirling (league match) 49,118
European record for a fourth-tier tie.

Every Rangers fan knows they have joined something larger when they are introduced to the club and not a single one will ever forget the details of that first game attended or watched, the memories of those who may no longer be with us and feeling we were in this for life. Not for nothing do the say you are born 'a Ger'.

A tribe in red, white and blue, born on the banks of the Clyde has rolled across the earth with open arms and built a worldwide legacy.

73

9IAR

For a generation of Rangers fans, the official Rangers VHS was a must-have (for younger readers a VHS was a video cassette tape!). Many will recall the image of a Rangers supporting dad speaking to his little boy:

'Can you not sleep son?' asks the concerned father, 'Tell me about nine-in-a-row,' replies the son.

Well, it goes like this:

Managed firstly by Graeme Souness and then Walter Smith, Rangers won nine consecutive Scottish league championships between 1989 and 1997, in the process equalling the Scottish record. It was a glorious era for the club as they swept all challenges aside and turned Scotland red, white and blue for a decade.

A cast of famous names: Woods, Butcher, Durrant, Steven, Hateley, Goram, Wilkins, Cooper, Cohen and many more all played a huge part. Notably the only three players who can lay claim to having the full set of nine winners' medals are Ally McCoist, Richard Gough and Ian Ferguson.

(League table finishes, see overleaf)

League Table Finishes – 9 In a Row

Season	Champions	Points	Runners-Up	Points
1988/89	Rangers	56	Aberdeen	50
1989/90	Rangers	51	Aberdeen	44
1990/91	Rangers	55	Aberdeen	53
1991/92	Rangers	72	Hearts	63
1992/93	Rangers	73	Aberdeen	64
1993/94	Rangers	58	Aberdeen	55
1994/95	Rangers	69	Motherwell	54
1995/96	Rangers	87	Celtic	83
1996/97	Rangers	80	Celtic	75

It remains one of the most fabulous periods in the club's history, a golden era when Rangers were rightly known as the footballing kings of Scotland. What a story that dad had to tell.

74

Tore Andre Flo –
Heavy Hangs the Price Tag

Heavy hangs the head that wears the price tag. That butchering of Shakespeare's Henry aside the point stands in particular relevance to striker Tore Andre Flo.

Before transfer fees outweighed the GDP of small nations, Rangers owner David Murray and manager Dick Advocaat doubled the Scottish transfer record in November 2000 by signing Chelsea striker Flo for £12m leading to charges from the Scottish media of Rangers being 'fat cats' and having an 'unfair advantage'.

Rangers at the time were 15 points behind in the title race and three days from an Old Firm game when the Norwegian international signed. In that Sunday game he would score, and Rangers would win 5-1, setting expectations high, reasonable given the spend and Flo's previous form for his old club.

But with such a price tag, allied to the demands of the Rangers support and in a declining team, could a player ever live up to the hype? Despite some good performances, and scoring 35 goals in 68 appearances, in the process winning both a Scottish and a League Cup winners medal there was always a feeling of unfilled promise, undefinable expectation.

He was moved to Sunderland in the 2002/03 season for

roughly half what Rangers had paid and remains, somewhat unfairly, the poster boy for the financial intransigence which came to define the David Murray era.

Tore Andre Flo celebrates his second goal against Hibs at Ibrox during the 2002 Scottish Cup run. *Alamy*

75

Employee Benefit Trust – EBT

What is an EBT and why does it feature in a book about Rangers? Well, the why is easily answered. You can bet your mortgage that when discussing Scottish football with rival fans, the term 'EBT' will come up. It is a fixation, one which has even led Celtic fans to produce movies and take out foreign newspaper adverts; talk about obsessed!

The what is slightly more complicated. An EBT was a legitimate tax vehicle employers could use to reduce the tax owed to HMRC on wages by paying loans into a players' trust instead of direct to the players themselves. This was very much tax avoidance, as opposed to the illegal act of tax evasion.

Rangers used the scheme between 2001 and 2010, as did many other clubs across Britain. However, in the run-up to the club's holding company liquidation HMRC challenged these trusts' validity and purported Rangers owed up to £74m (including EBT payments, interest and penalty charges).

At the time, and subsequently, HMRC's handling of the affair was seen by supporters to have affected the potential sale of the club with investors scared off by a potentially huge bill. HMRC finally admitted to serious mistakes in their calculations, dropping claims against former players along the way.

Rangers' fans were left with a feeling of anger and 'what if' over the effect a clearer picture sooner could have had on saving the holding company, whilst calls for an independent inquiry into that, as well as suspected media leaks from the revenue service, refuse to go away. The Scottish Lord Advocates Office has also had cause to apologise for its handling of the case.

76

Auchenhowie

It may seem unbelievable that there was a time in the not-so-distant past when the Rangers first-team squad had to get changed at Ibrox and then jump in a minibus to go to training on hired pitches. Not what you'd expect from Scotland's biggest club and an eye-opener for new signings.

That all changed when Dutch manager Dick Advocaat convinced David Murray to build a state-of-the-art training facility in a much-needed move to bring the club into the modern era. It was not the only upgrade Advocaat brought, with his teams playing arguably the greatest football ever seen at Ibrox.

Originally named somewhat narcissistically as 'Murray Park' but now known as Auchenhowie, the facility cost an initial £14m when it was unveiled in July 2001.

Covering an initial 38 acres it included six full-size pitches, two half-size, an indoor pitch and training centre.

Reinvented and refreshed several times the centre is now home to the men's, women's and youth teams and continues its state-of-the-art edge with a cryogenic chamber to aid player injury recovery, a fan-paid-for stand, recovery rooms, intelligent gym equipment linked to an in-house computer system with personalised player settings as well as a hydro pool and player analytics suites to help identify targets.

Used by visiting top European and international sides, the centre has also helped shape the careers of the likes of Barry Ferguson, Alan Hutton, John Fleck and Billy Gilmour and has been pivotal in helping to lure top talent to the club.

77

Blue Heaven

To coincide with the opening of the Auchenhowie training centre (known as Murray Park at the time) Rangers commissioned the filming of a six-part television series called *Blue Heaven*. The show documented the journey of a group of young footballers as they tried to make the breakthrough at the club.

Filmed over two years, the series covered the end of Dick Advocaat's tenure and the beginning of the McLeish era. A follow-up episode was broadcast in May 2011.

Notable players who were part of the filming and would go on to make an impact in the first team included Charlie Adam, Chris Burke and Steven Smith, whilst others unfortunately did not make the grade and were released.

An innovation ahead of its time before behind-the-scenes football documentaries became a go-to for many channels.

78

Hall of Fame, Beyond Football

Some players embody more than just the game they are destined to play, they are recognised for a transcendent talent and their ability to inspire both on and off the field.

Only three former Rangers have had the honour of being inducted into the Scottish Sports Hall of Fame:

Name	Date Inducted
Jim Baxter	2002
John Greig	2002
Ally McCoist	2007

79

Das Boot

As you look through the riches in the Ibrox trophy room it is impossible not to notice a magnificent red-white-and-blue model fishing trawler inside a large glass case, the good ship PFC *Balmoor*. Or perhaps that should be HMS *Balmoor*.

Gifts between clubs are part of the fabric and tradition of the game and the directors of Peterhead Football Club, or to know them by their nickname 'the Blue Toon', outdid themselves with this one.

Finely detailed, the gift was presented when Rangers hosted Peterhead at Ibrox on 7 January 2006 in a Scottish Cup third round match.

Unfortunately for Peterhead their hopes of progression in the tournament were sunk with Rangers coasting to a 5-0 victory against the lower league side. A near 40,000 crowd also saw new signing Kris Boyd score a debut hat-trick following his arrival from Kilmarnock. A penalty, predatory penalty box finish and header set the tone for the man who would go on to score numerous goals for the club and score a double and covert in a penalty shoot-out (albeit in the CIS Cup Final) in an epic 3-2 win over Dundee United in 2008.

80

Sky Rocker

Heavy metal is not a phrase you probably want to hear in connection with your air travel, but it is exactly what Rangers encountered on their charter flight to play Israel's Hapoel Tel Aviv in 2007.

Bruce Dickinson, frontman for rock group Iron Maiden, famous for hits such as 'Bring Your Daughter to the Slaughter', 'Run to the Hills', 'The Number of the Beast' and 'The Trooper' is a qualified commercial pilot and often took the controls on long-haul flights, unknown to passengers. But on this occasion, he specifically asked to fly when he heard he had a chance to put the blue in 'blue skies'.

Rangers manager Walter Smith told the club's website at the time: 'I know their stuff quite well. I remember going to meet the band when they played in Edinburgh a few years ago but I would never have thought that Bruce would be flying our plane.'

The Gers would lose the match 2-1 but would turn in a great 4-0 performance in the second leg at Ibrox to progress to the next round of 16, 5-2 on aggregate. Next up would be Osasuna who would end Rangers' involvement, squeezing past thanks to a 1-1 draw at Ibrox and a 1-0 win in Spain. More was to come from the light blues in the UEFA Cup the following season.

81

Formula Rangers

Rangers fans are used to seeing the team speeding ahead of their rivals, but not usually at over 100mph!

In 2008, Rangers revealed that their car would compete in the Superleague Formula racing league against teams such as Atlético Madrid and PSV Eindhoven.

Despite some impressive performances, the team, overseen by Alan Docking Racing, was unable to finish first in any of their races across either the 2008 or 2009 seasons, after which Rangers ended their association.

The Superleague is now defunct but for those two years Rangers were certainly the fastest club in Scotland!

82

UEFA Cup Final – 2008

Rangers started their journey towards an eventual appearance in a UEFA Cup Final in the Champions League. A stand-out result, winning 3-0 away in Lyon, couldn't prevent them from finishing third and dropping into the UEFA Cup.

Greek side Panathinaikos were beaten on away goals after two stodgy draws, 0-0 at Ibrox and 1-1 in Greece.

The next round of 16 saw German cracks Werder Bremen dispatched, Rangers keeper Allan McGregor making one of the all-time great saves to deny a point-blank certain goal. A quarter-final tie against Sporting Lisbon was navigated, Steven Whittaker scoring one of the goals of the season with a mazy run from the halfway line in the away tie before neatly finishing past the keeper. Next up came Italy's Fiorentina who were sent crashing out after two tense ties and an energy-sapping penalty shoot-out. Rangers Nacho Novo scored the all-important kick to send the away fans into ecstasy.

And so, 36 years after their last European cup final appearance, Rangers fans descended on Manchester (host city of the final) in their hundreds of thousands. On a bakingly hot May afternoon Rangers fans overtook an entire city. Squares were packed, bars drunk dry, even 40,000 packed Ibrox back home to watch a beam back of the game.

Ex-Rangers manager Dick Advocaat was manager of opponents

Zenit St Petersburg, the free-spending Russians being tipped as favourites. In a tense affair Zenit broke the deadlock late on before adding a second in injury time to crush light-blue hopes.

Slightly soured by the disorder of a minority of fans in the aftermath of the result, the team had confounded all expectations and given a lifetime of memories.

Almost harder to swallow than the result was the lack of support from the national footballing body. Whilst the Russian FA had league fixtures moved to help Zenit prepare for the final, the Scottish authorities refused such support when asked, making Rangers play four days before the final. A point not forgotten or forgiven by the fans to this day.

The team line up before the 2008 UEFA Cup Final against Zenit St Petersburg in Manchester. *Alamy*

83

Nine of the Rangers is all you need

Victory, victory against all the odds. That's the essence of football. 11 v 11, or if you are the famous Glasgow Rangers, let's make it 11 of you and 9 of us in a cup final to keep it interesting!

The 2010 CIS Co-operative Cup Final was played on a lovely March afternoon, the sun pouring over the majority Rangers 44,518 crowd. Red, white and blue appeared to be Hampden Park's official colours.

Rangers were up against plucky underdogs St Mirren under manager Gus McPherson (who at one time had been at Rangers in his playing days, never quite making the grade), going for a potential domestic treble against the backdrop of financial uncertainty, with back and front pages in the build-up dominated by the collapse of the bid by businessman Andrew Ellis to buy the club. But this was a Rangers fashioned by the legendary Walter Smith, so hopes were high and financial worries forgotten for 90 minutes.

The first half of the game was largely dominated by St Mirren, with Rangers happy to soak up any pressure, secure in their defensive capabilities; 0-0 at half-time and everything to play for, two teams with 45 minutes to claim the prize, surely Rangers for the win?

Well, that became a whole lot more difficult when Kevin Thomson snapped into a tackle in the 52nd minute. Straight red. Ten-man Rangers against an uplifted St Mirren.

More pressure, but the 'Paisley buddies' remained unable to unlock the Gers' backline until a long ball over the top in the 70th minute when young centre-back Danny Wilson was caught wrong side and fouled to a goalscoring opportunity. Second red card for Rangers and down to nine men!

Twenty minutes left on the clock, 9 vs 11, Rangers up against it, the fans disbelieving but the score line still 0-0. Never would a small club get a better chance to beat Rangers in a major final.

Resolute defending, blue jerseys scrambling along the defensive ramparts of the 18- and six-yard boxes. The blue line holding.

Then the unimaginable 83rd minute. A St Mirren attack breaks down, captain Davie Weir strides out of the backline before forcing the ball on to Steven Naismith surging up the right wing. Surely not.

Naismith carries on toward the Saints box, Rangers fans beginning to stand, roaring the tired legs of strikers Nacho Novo and Kenny Miller on as they make their respective predatory runs.

In comes the cross, met sweetly by the head of Miller and beyond the despairing goalkeeper. One-nil to the nine men!

St Mirren tried to pile on the pressure, but it was clear their players were shellshocked and didn't quite believe they could get back level. Rangers had sapped their will. Then the final whistle, rapture in red, white and blue. The image of Smith on the touchline arm raised, fist clenched is one burned into the memory.

A 26th League Cup against all the odds. Rangers would repeat a similar feat in the 2018 Europa League qualifying play-off second leg against Russians Ufa, going down to nine men but grinding out a 1-1 draw on the night to go through 2-1 on aggregate.

At Rangers though, the only numbers that really matter are the trophies won.

84

Craig Whyte

Craig Whyte was infamously once described by a tabloid hack as having 'wealth off the radar'. This was true in that the wealth couldn't be spotted by radar, sonar, sight or any other physical process . . .

He managed to put himself at the front of the queue when David Murray decided to sell his controlling stake in the club given the debt pressures he had burdened it with, a potential tax bill of £49m, and Lloyds Banking Group demanding action on monies they were owed. Ultimately ownership of the grandest and most storied club in Scotland passed to Whyte for a meagre £1.

This was in May 2011 and there were already significant concerns amongst the blue faithful about Whyte's ability to deliver on his promises. On Valentine's Day 2012 those fears would be realised as Whyte placed the club into administration over a PAYE bill of £9m.

It then emerged Whyte had only been able to fund the entire takeover deal (including promises of player investment to then manager Ally McCoist) by mortgaging future season ticket sales with the help of London-based financial outfit Ticketus.

To add to this, the SFA fined Whyte £200,000 and banned him from Scottish football for life for bringing the game into disrepute when it came to light he had neglected to disclose he had been disqualified from holding directorships of any company for seven years in 2000.

On 12 June, Rangers fans' fears were realised when HMRC announced they would reject the CVA proposal and force the club into liquidation.

The sharks of Scottish football started to circle as it became clear Rangers were on their knees. A transfer embargo and points deduction were forced upon the club with some calling for titles to be handed back due to the club's tax affairs (more on that later).

A villain in the eyes of all Rangers supporters to this day, it remains a complex mystery how Whyte was able to successfully gain ownership of the club and damage such an institution. In time Rangers would recover, but it is doubtful that Whyte's reputation among Rangers fans ever will.

85

A Baw in a Hedge

Many a child will testify to the danger of their football getting trapped atop a high hedge; it can be a real game killer if you do not have a tall friend or a stick. But in a professional game, surely not!

Such is the lasting image from Rangers' game away to Brechin City at Glebe Park in the Ramsden's Cup in 2012.

Rangers were there due to their financial implosion and demotion to the lower orders following the holding company's liquidation and subsequent last-minute agreement to offer the club a conditional entry to the Scottish Football League.

Rangers fans flooded the area in their thousands, intent on showing the players, and anyone else watching, that the club might have lost its top-flight status, but it certainly had not lost the loyalty of the blue legions. One fan taking it slightly too far and climbing a floodlight to the delight of the away support.

Brechin, like all Scottish clubs, know the value of the Rangers support to their coffers. They sold commemorative mugs and badges and produced a special on-off edition of their discontinued matchday programme.

The game was fairly rudimentary with a hastily assembled Rangers side requiring a Lee McCulloch goal to see off Brechin in extra time and manager McCoist stating, 'Like any cup tie, you just need to get through. That was our first competitive game, and we were just pleased to get the opportunity to play.'

But that image of the ball stuck on top of the hedge in the 36th minute was a fitting one for what the Rangers support refer to as 'the journey' or, more jocularly, 'the banter years'.

The hedge itself never turned pro, although it is fair to say it had a better ability to trap a ball than some of the players who would do injustice to the blue jersey for the next few seasons.

© Alamy

86

Implosion

In 2012, on Valentine's Day, owner Craig Whyte placed the club into administration and, in an act of historical vandalism, allowed the holding company to be liquidated and the club relegated.

What followed was a tawdry spectacle of smaller clubs, long in Rangers' shadow, clamouring for the club to be demoted and stripped of titles won in the years EBTs were used. This included the governing bodies of Scottish football, who perversely wished to insert this into what would become known as the 'five-way agreement'. This agreement was the vehicle by which league membership would transfer from the old holding company (now liquidated) to the new.

Men like Ally McCoist and Sandy Jardine deserve great praise for their actions during this period; their robust defence saved the club from losing titles in boardrooms that their rivals could not win on the pitch.

In 2012 Lord Nimmo Smith, appointed as independent chair into the investigation by the SPL (Scottish Premier League) on the use of EBTs, ruled they were legitimate. He also confirmed the stance of the European Club Association (ECA) that Rangers 'the club' has an unbroken history. Rangers' holding company may have been liquidated, but the club's history remained intact.

A salutary lesson in the dangers of modern football finance, it was only by the defence of the club from those within and without that its soul and history were saved.

87

The Gazebo

Mistrust, disbelief and disaffection. Is it possible for a construction to have these personality traits or at least to be the epitome of them? Rangers fans certainly thought so back in December 2014 as they filed into the club AGM and spotted a gazebo placed a fair distance away from their seats in the corner of the Broomloan and Sandy Jardine stands.

With the demotion and despair of 2012, Rangers' financial and boardroom situation became the anthesis of what the club values had been. Gone were the quiet dignity of high standards and good governance, replaced by a soap opera succession of owners and directors whose interest in the club beyond its sellable assets was questionable.

Disquiet and disaffection amongst the support quickly became apparent, even more so when it became public knowledge that businessman and Newcastle United owner Mike Ashley had become involved in the club against most fans' wishes, having his man Derek Llambias appointed Chief Executive.

The 2014 AGM was a tense affair, with fans booing everyone but keeping the brunt of their displeasure for David Somers, Derek Llambias, James Easdale and club chairman Sandy Easdale.

Tired of being told to 'settle down' or that 'when you're chairman of Rangers, you can do it your way', the fans (alongside former player John Brown and future 'Three Bear' Paul Murray) attempted to get an understanding of the make-up of the club's fragile financial state, the direction of recovery and the transparency required to build bridges. None was forthcoming.

A temporary shelter, the tent would soon be blown away by the blue winds of change as the group known collectively (and somewhat tritely) as the three bears, with Dave King moved in to enact regime change and give the fans people they could place real trust and belief in. Many club AGMs have taken place since, and thankfully for fans, never a gazebo in sight.

88

The Three Bears and Dave King

The phrase 'Three Bears' may evoke childhood fairy tales but for Rangers fans the need for their existence was much more of a nightmare.

Following the club's demotion to the lowest tier in Scottish football in 2012 on the back of financial implosion, Rangers fell into the hands of asset strippers, charlatans and carpet-baggers.

Standards long fought for and held dear were replaced with short-term soundbites and glib understandings of the weight custodianship of an institution Rangers' size brings.

In 2015, control was finally wrested back with the help of three businessmen fans could back. Douglas Park, John Gilligan and George Letham are rightly considered as saviours of the club at a time when it had few friends and a bleak future.

Still attached to the club, their investment and action helped set the stage for a return to disciplined ownership and governance.

In support of the group and principal among them was South-African based businessman Dave King who had previously invested in Rangers in the David Murray era. His financial weight, aggressive style and determination were key in securing the club, de-shackling it from the jackals and progressing a modern business model. He stepped away from the club in 2020, leaving with the goodwill and thanks of a grateful Ibrox faithful.

89

'Tav'

What defines a Rangers captain? Grit? Determination? Class? Winning?

Current captain James Tavernier has had to show all these qualities and more during his time at the club, in the process losing and then regaining the trust and support of the blue legions.

Brought to the club by Mark Warburton from English side Wigan in 2015, when Rangers were in the second tier of Scottish football, he started in fantastic fashion, scoring a stunning debut free kick in a 6-2 humbling of Edinburgh side Hibs.

Rangers were promoted in that first season, Tavernier assisting the cause with 15 goals, although the campaign ended painfully as Hibs gained revenge by beating the Gers 3-2 in the Scottish Cup Final with a last-minute header. Tavernier was rightly blamed by large sections of the support and media for some inept defending.

He also had to contend with being a focal point during the period when Rangers were rebuilding after financial implosion and rivals Celtic were enjoying unprecedented success. He was part of some humiliating defeats against the club's Glasgow foes; Celtic scoring five goals was not uncommon as Rangers toiled under stuttering managers and sub-standard squads whilst lurching from crisis to crisis. This was a tough period for the

fans and some players could not handle the pressure brought by wearing the Rangers crest.

However, 'Tav' carried on and when Steven Gerrard swept into power in 2018, he was made captain of the club, joining the ranks of Gough and Greig. But still the mistakes came, often through lack of back-post defending, as did the wait for a trophy. There was progress, however, both at home and abroad as the full-back grew with his new, improved teammates and coach.

In 2021 Rangers, captained by James Tavernier, won their 55th league championship, in the process stopping Celtic's attempt for ten titles in a row. Front and centre, wearing the armband was Tav, his hands holding aloft the craved-for silverware.

In the process of that season his team had broken multiple records, including number of clean sheets maintained and the earliest date the league had been won by. In amongst his defensive duties, he also found time to continue his swashbuckling marauding style, adding 11 league goals and ten assists which saw him end the season as the club's top scorer overall as well being voted PFA Scotland Player of the Year. An incredible tale of determination and will to win. Tav grew into the shirt and can now rightfully lay claim to being a winning Rangers captain.

Opposite: James Tavernier with the Scottish Premiership trophy at Ibrox after the club sealed its 55th title in 2021. *Alamy*

90

The Bush – Progrés Niederkorn

There aren't many famous bushes. There is the burning one from the Bible, the American presidents and, well, that's it really. But Rangers' history has one in all its leafy glory (and that is the only reference to glory within this object).

Picture the scene, a balmy July evening in Luxembourg. Anger in the air as a suited man argues with a crowd of incensed supporters whilst standing amidst shrubbery, a club official attempting to coax him out of the foliage.

The man was Rangers manager Pedro Caixinha, furiously remonstrating with travelling fans having just seen his team dumped out of Europa League qualification by the part-timers of Progrés Niederkorn. A 2-0 humbling from a team who had never won a game at European level and had managed one goal in 13 previous ties.

Caixinha was heralded as a new era for Rangers, the next move forward following some tough times. To then oversee such a result set a tone and produced a toxic atmosphere between the manager and the fans.

Almost any fan will tell you this was the club's worst result ever. The bush, however, declined to comment.

91

Pedro PowerPoint

A Microsoft PowerPoint presentation, so the popular story goes, is how Portuguese manager Pedro Caixinha (of the Luxembourg bush fame) came to wow the Rangers board and secure himself the manager's job. However, there was immediate talk of a boardroom split on his appointment.

Now this may be unfair on Pedro and the board. Caixinha was a qualified professional manager who had managed or been assistant manager in Europe, Mexico and the Middle East before being handed the opportunity to become Rangers' 16th permanent manager since their formation (in an era of manager merry-go-round you read that correctly).

He was managing Qatari side Al-Gharafa when he was introduced by agent (and former Rangers player) Pedro Mendes to the Rangers board. He won over the selection committee and was brought in on a three-year deal to turn around the club's fortunes (with a reported £300,000 paid in compensation to his former club.

Despite his debut in the dugout being a 4-0 victory over Hamilton Academicals there was little substance behind the promise and his side set all the wrong type of records. Ignominy in Europe against part-timers, a record 5-1 defeat against arch-rivals Celtic at Ibrox, a comprehensive demolition by Celtic again in the Scottish Cup (4-0) as well as being beaten by Aberdeen at Ibrox (the first time this had happened in 26 years) as well as a shambolic Betfred Cup semi-final defeat to Motherwell all followed.

It was no surprise to the majority of the support, when, following a poor 1-1 draw against Kilmarnock at Ibrox, leaving Rangers in fourth place in the league (which included a never-before-seen red card intervention by the fourth official) and with reported player unrest that Caixinha's tenure was brought to a close after only seven months.

No comment has been made on whether the PowerPoint slides were recycled.

92

El Bufalo

In the modern era it is unsurprising to see players play in multiple countries, unlike almost any other profession, football is a global endeavour. However, arriving in Govan from the heart of South America via Finland must still be something of an eye-opener.

But goals are borderless and young Alfredo Morelos, growing up poverty stricken in Cereté, Colombia, had the dream of raising himself and his family up through his talent. Starting at Independiente Medellín he established himself, even breaking into the Colombia U21 national squad before Finland's HJK Helsinki came calling.

Many 20-year-olds would be fazed by the cultural differences and challenges, not to mention the weather difference a 6,000km journey brings!

Morelos isn't that kind of person, however. 'Buff' was up for the challenge, driven by that need to support his family and community. It led to him storming the Finnish league, firing HJK to the title with 47 goals in 62 appearances.

In June 2017 then Rangers manager Pedro Caixinha (in one of his few positive legacies) brought the striker to Ibrox for £1m, a relatively small fee in global football terms but large for Rangers given their contextual financial position. It would be money very well spent.

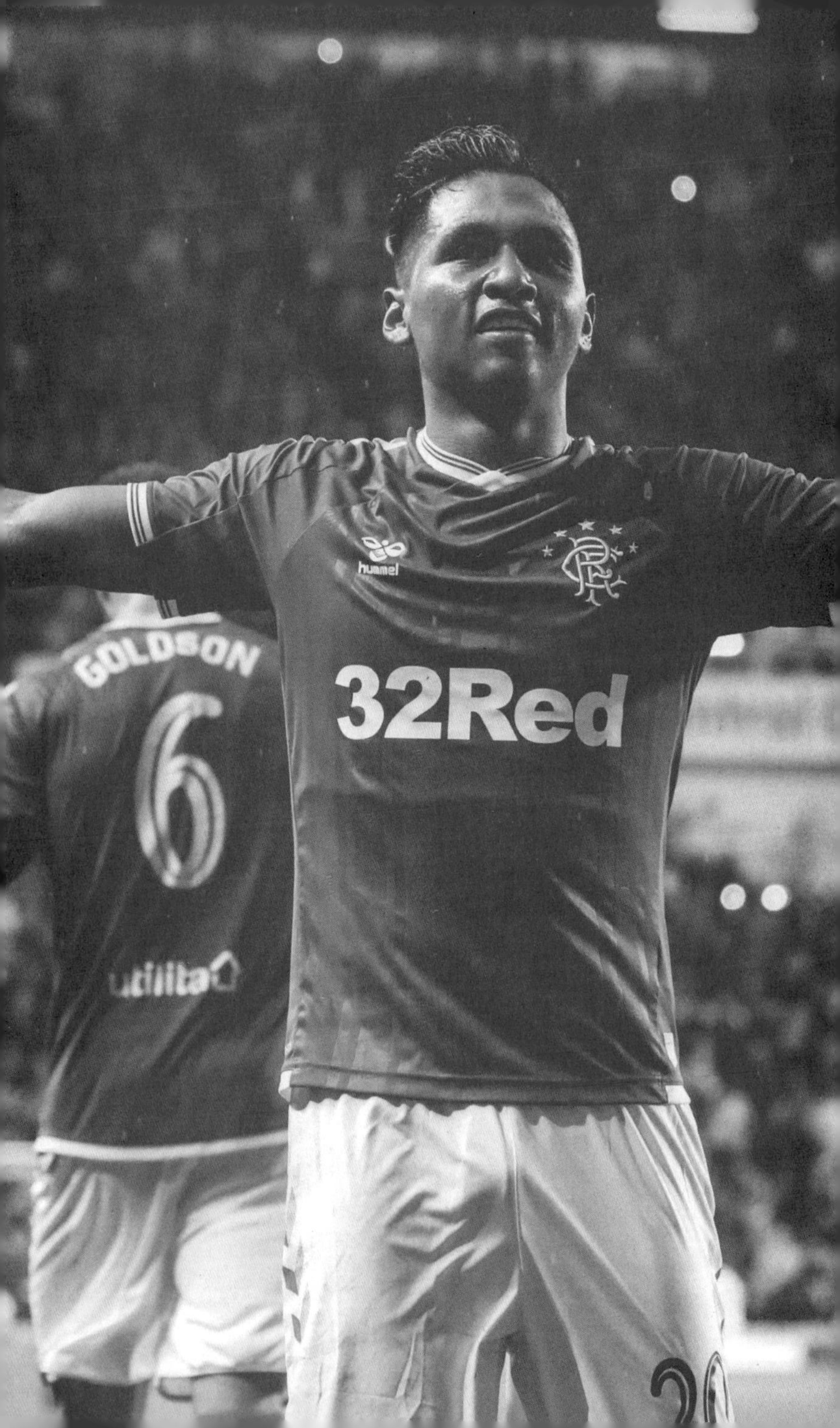
hummel
32Red
GOLDSON
6
utilita

Branded a 'hot-head' by the Scottish media due to initial (somewhat unfair) disciplinary issues, Morelos has had to endure racist abuse and derogatory comments about his family from rival fans as well as being linked to lazy stereotypical Colombian narratives about the drugs trade by tabloid journalists. He has stayed quiet, in the process beating Ally McCoist's European goalscoring record, setting a European record for goals scored in European tournaments pre-Christmas (14), finishing as the club's top scorer, netting against Celtic after a drought of 14 games and most importantly winning the club's coveted 55th league championship.

Undoubtedly Rangers will eventually cash in on the player and he will go with the best wishes of the fans. It is that relationship which has defined his time with the club. In a period where Rangers were still rebuilding to former glory, Morelos was an embodiment of the underdog, the passion, drive, commitment and desire to win. The support took to him and he them; his is a journey to match that taken by the club since financial implosion.

El Bufalo, from the heart of Colombia.

93

Steven Gerrard

A first-time manager who also happens to be a Liverpool legend? No, you haven't slipped back to reading about Graeme Souness. This time Rangers reached directly into Merseyside for the man they believed could deliver them the title.

Gerrard had been coaching the Liverpool under-18 squad when majority shareholder Dave King and then Director of Football Mark Allen convinced him to take the Ibrox job in 2018. He inherited a divided club and sub-standard squad but was convinced he was the man to end Celtic's domestic dominance.

Galvanising the club from top to bottom he instilled a sense of pride and a return to the standards which have underpinned its success.

Pride in Europe was rediscovered due to notable runs in the UEFA Europa League, but two seasons passed without any silverware.

In the 2020/21 season, Celtic looked to go one better than Rangers and secure their tenth successive league title. Could Gerrard avoid this misery being inflicted on the Rangers support and in doing so give them a first title since 2011?

His and his players' answer was an emphatic yes, smashing Celtic's grip so thoroughly the league was won in the earliest-ever timescale (March).

One trophy from nine domestic attempts is not the stuff of greatness on paper, although that is to misunderstand the power of becoming champions in a city riven with rivalry.

Gerrard is just beginning his managerial career and has a long way to go to emulate the likes of Waddell, Smith or Struth but crushing the decade-long-held dreams of your main rival is not a bad way to begin!

© Alamy

94

A Story to Tell

With a story almost 150 years in the making, and with no sign of stopping soon, it is hardly surprising Rangers have lots of tales to tell and this book is a small homage to that.

But space is limited within the stadium, including in the iconic Blue and Trophy rooms. So, what to do, how does the club tell that story and (in the modern age extremely important) also generate revenue. A museum dedicated to the club, the fans and its history, that's how.

In 2019, managing director Stewart Robertson announced to fans the club were looking at ways to update and deliver on the club's stadium footprint (this is modern talk for the area round the stadium). Fast forward to 2021 and detailed plans for the demolishing and rebuilding of the dilapidated Edmiston House (opposite the stadium) to introduce 'New Edmiston House' which would, along with the museum, add a concert space to the local area (Glasgow being renowned for both its football and musical heritage).

It cannot be overlooked that for so long the fans of this great club have had no way to engage with their collective history, shared passion and community outside of matchdays. To have a space dedicated to those who have gone before should help energise new generations to recognise why one of Rangers' many nicknames is 'the Famous'.

Some stories need to be told, and here, in the shadow of the stadium, when opened, fans both old and new can mix with tourists unconnected to Rangers and learn how a dream of four young lads evolved through triumph, loss and tragedy and led to the world's most successful football team.

95

Digitally Native

Much has changed since the club's formation in 1872; notably we now live in the 'digital' era with the web, smartphones and social media ever-present in our lives.

In July 2020 Rangers decided to join the party with a refreshed on-line presence which included a makeover for the club crest and a new Rangers font as the club, as they put it, moved to be 'digitally native' (which sounds like an indigenous on-line tribe). In an increasingly crowded on-line world, with influencers, content and clickbait all fighting for attention, it is important Rangers' brand remains vibrant and able to attract people, their support and, in a pragmatist's view, their money.

A club crest is not something to be toyed with lightly, it is a symbol of the history and glory, the heraldry of collective cause against all comers. Rangers', with its rampant lion (a lion standing on hind legs), emblazoned on a ball with the words 'Rangers Football Club' and 'Ready' circling it is one of the most recognisable in world football.

Rangers sharpened the image (and claws) of the lion, moved the wording and also became the first club in world football to introduce its own font.

It is not the only crest the club has, there is also the 'star crest' and the 'scroll crest' and the 2021 150th year 'anniversary crest' but the refreshed crest will be the one surfers of the web see.

Change is never easy, and some fans were less than complimentary; however, the majority realise Rangers should always look to be at the forefront of modern developments, ever 'Ready' you might say.

96

Braga Comeback

The comeback is the greatest feeling in football, to see your team come back from certain defeat is unrivalled. To do so in Europe after a decade of trauma is the stuff of dreams.

So, imagine Rangers supporters' high at the final whistle following a pulsating match at Ibrox in the UEFA Europa League against Portuguese high-flyers Braga on a rainy Glasgow February evening in 2020.

Braga were dominant initially, pulling Rangers across the pitch, opening gaps and creating chances. It was no real surprise when Brazilian midfielder Fransérgio strode forward and smashed a swerving 25-yard drive in off the crossbar. Even less so when Abel Ruiz, on loan from Spanish giants Barcelona, created space on the edge of the box and powered low beyond Allan McGregor. The Gers were 2-0 down.

But there is fire down Govan way and something, or someone, lit the spark. Ianis Hagi, son of the famous and fabulously talented Gheorghe. He picked up a Steven Davis pass wide on the right, cut inside and lashed the ball in off the post. One goal back and the Ibrox roar began, Braga looked shaken, Rangers looked like they believed.

The fans turned up the noise level, willing the team on before Joe Aribo somehow evaded five challenges before levelling the match. Pandemonium in the stands.

Fittingly, Hagi, who had sparked Rangers into life, had the final say. The Romanian's free kick from 25 yards was deflected, wrong-footing Matheus in the Braga goal. 3-2 Rangers and that pandemonium moved into the stratosphere.

At the final whistle a roar rolled out from the stands; this wasn't just a comeback, it was one of those glittering European nights that harked back to Rangers' past, so impossible during the years of demotion. A reset, a return to knowing Rangers had recovered their heart. As players and fans applauded each other's performance a connection solidified. This was a real Rangers team.

Ianis Hagi celebrates scoring Rangers' third goal against Braga at Ibrox. *Alamy*

97

Professional Parity – The Women's Game

Women players have long struggled to gain the recognition their talent and professionalism deserves in a male-dominated game. How pleasing that Rangers are now firmly recognised as being leaders in promoting the women's side of football.

In 2020 Rangers announced that they would become the first club in Scotland to have a full-time professional women's team. This was a bold move and backed by fully integrating the side into the same resources and facilities the men's first-team enjoyed.

It also spurred other clubs such as Celtic and Hearts to follow suit, further strengthening the commitment to women's football across Scotland.

2020/21 was the team's first season, and despite some good results they were unable to overcome eventual champions Glasgow City, finishing third. But success takes time; importantly the players know they are at a club that takes the women's game seriously and the fans can look forward to being able to support another Rangers team.

98

Fan Media

As noted previously in this book, fans (and rivals) have always had a fascination with the goings-on at Rangers. The workings, the players, gossip, signings, all is grist to the media mill.

These days the advent of 'fan media' has provided outlets for the club, both officially and unofficially, whilst allowing fans a direct ability to interact with the club and each other.

Rangers have a particularly vibrant fan media landscape with notables such as *This Is Ibrox*, *Heart and Hand* and the blog *Four Lads Had a Dream* as well as a host of others all giving more 'traditional' media challenges when it comes to owning the reporting narrative.

The trajectory of fan media, however, does appear to be moving toward traditional subscription methods and, as with any media, the challenges content-providing 'fans' will face will be retaining objectivity and fairness when discussing the club they support as well as maintaining good relations with an increasingly revenue-orientated club media relations department.

If they can achieve this, then fans can harness mass media to ensure transparency and accountability from those who purport to be custodians of the club and its values.

For the club, the balance will be in utilising fan media well without locking out those fans who cannot afford mass subscriptions. This is even more important as the club now demands media outlets (including fan media) pay up to £25k per season for media access to press conferences and players.

99

The League Championship

Scotland's national league trophy is, these days at least, the one every club wants to win. It is the barometer of success, the gold standard, or silver if you will.

First played for in the 1890/91 season, Abercorn, Cambuslang, Celtic, Cowlairs, Dumbarton, Hearts, Rangers, Renton, St Bernard's, St Mirren, Third Lanark and Vale of Leven all vied for the inaugural crown with Rangers and Dumbarton eventually sharing the trophy that, standing 24 inches high, proudly bore the words 'Scottish Football League Division One Championship'.

With the resumption of football after the Second World War in season 1946/47, the leagues were renamed the A or B Division but the original trophy was still awarded to the champions of Division A. In 1956 the leagues were renamed Divisions One and Two, again returning to the pre-war categorisation.

Through reconstruction in the 1975/76 season, the trophy was used for the new 'Premier Division' despite its 'Division One' inscription. Following the end of season 1997/98 the Premier Division clubs of Scotland (including Rangers of course) broke away to form the new Scottish Premier League at which time a newly commissioned trophy for the SPL championship was installed leading to the original 1891 trophy being given (as it still is) to the winners of the second-tier league.

Rangers have been synonymous with league victory since the league's inception and have seen wonderful last-day wins (and the odd loss), securing a world-record 55 titles all in (this is outwith titles won during the war years which Rangers, unlike some rival clubs, do not count officially). This includes an incredible nine-in-a-row between 1989 and 1997. And yes, more on both that nine and that 55th later.

Nothing is more guaranteed to gladden the supporters' hearts than the sight of the league trophy with red, white and blue ribbons tied on. Judging by the stats it is the trophy's preferred look!

55 times the Kings of Scotland:

1891*, 1899, 1900, 1901, 1902, 1911, 1912, 1913, 1918, 1920, 1921, 1923, 1924, 1925, 1927, 1928, 1929, 1930, 1931, 1933, 1934, 1935, 1937, 1939, 1947, 1949, 1950, 1953, 1956, 1957, 1959, 1961, 1963, 1964, 1975, 1976, 1978, 1987, 1989, 1990, 1991, 1992, 1993, 1994, 1995, 1996, 1997, 1999, 2000, 2003, 2005, 2009, 2010, 2011, 2021

*Shared with Dumbarton

100

55

When Rangers took to the field against Aberdeen on the opening day of the 2020/21 season, they knew it was a numbers game.

Would it end with the long-wished for 55th league championship or would Celtic fans be celebrating ten-in-a-row? Someone's dream had to die.

Rangers set an early pace, showing a new defensive fortitude and in the process racking up clean sheet after clean sheet. Captain James Tavernier, ever-present centre-back Connor Goldson and goalkeeper Allan McGregor deserving special praise in a squad who were all performing at their peak.

An early defeat of Celtic at Parkhead in October (2-0) set the tone. Rangers were here to deliver. Following that game, they would score 21 goals, conceding one in their next six games as teams were swotted aside.

Old Firm day again smiled on Rangers on 2 January as they managed to take all three points without having a shot on target, Celtic's Callum McGregor temporarily forgetting his loyalties with an own goal.

Celtic imploded, manager Neil Lennon sacked after a disastrous run left Hoops fans hoping for league closure due to the COVID-19 pandemic. They were to be disappointed.

Rangers remained relentless, refusing to be beaten by any challenger. Ibrox in particular was a graveyard for rival teams

(Rangers only conceded four goals there all season).

The title was duly delivered to euphoric scenes when a humiliated and demoralised Celtic could not beat Dundee United to maintain the façade of a challenge. A decade of hurt had been washed away, the liquidation, the journey, the satisfaction. They say that it is a cosmic truth the universe maintains natural order. It had been restored in Scotland, Rangers were champions.

The team would hand Celtic a 4-1 lesson in the final Old Firm match of the season, ensuring they went unbeaten against them for the first time since 2000. In the process they would also produce an 'invincible' season, going the entire league campaign without suffering defeat. A remarkable achievement in any season never mind the pressure cooker that this one was.

A season won in the fastest time by an invincible team who also set a clean-sheet record. It is fair to say in 2020/21 the 'Famous' turned up.

SCOTTISH PREMIERSHIP CHAMPIONS 20/21

101

To 150 and Beyond

In March 2021, Rangers unveiled their chosen crest to celebrate the upcoming 150th-year anniversary of the club.

On a sea of blue sits a gold crest, an unfurled scroll reading 1872 to 2022, the club's motto of 'ready' stands but in promotional material has been updated to 'Forever Ready'.

It is a huge milestone and a reminder of the history and legacy of the club, even more so when you consider that Rangers are Europe's first major club to be able to celebrate reaching 150.

The tapestry the club has woven in Glasgow and beyond is incomparable, families have lived with and for 'the Rangers', we have won and lost together, suffering tragedy and triumph in equally stoic fashion. The club's watchwords have been dignity and success.

Against all the odds, a dream of four penniless boys has become the most successful club of them all, and you'll find the blue flag flying high from Bathgate to Bangkok, Sydney to San Francisco.

A worldwide institution that retains its community feel, the global standard for success, born in Glasgow, raised in Govan.

The next 150 years should be just as historic.